TO ALEX:
WISHING you,
ROUTINE PERFECTION IN LIFE!

THE ART OF
ROUTINE

THE ART OF
ROUTINE

Discover How Routineology
Can Transform Your Life

ANGEL ISCOVICH, MD
WITH JOE GARNER AND MICHAEL ASHLEY

Skyhorse Publishing

Skyhorse Publishing books may be purchased in bulk at special discounts for sales promotion, corporate gifts, fund-raising, or educational purposes. Special editions can also be created to specifications. For details, contact the Special Sales Department, Skyhorse Publishing, 307 West 36th Street, 11th Floor, New York, NY 10018 or info@skyhorsepublishing.com.

Skyhorse® and Skyhorse Publishing® are registered trademarks of Skyhorse Publishing, Inc.®, a Delaware corporation.

Visit our website at www.skyhorsepublishing.com.

10 9 8 7 6 5 4 3 2 1

Library of Congress Cataloging-in-Publication Data is available on file.

Jacket design by Daniel Brount
Jacket illustration by Shutterstock

Print ISBN: 978-1-5107-6455-2
Ebook ISBN: 978-1-5107-6456-9

Printed in the United States of America

To my mother, Eva, who taught us that
"everyone has their own rainbow"

Table of Contents

CHAPTER 1

March Madness
in 2020

I USED TO PRACTICE EMERGENCY MEDICINE, working long shifts in hospital facilities for up to forty-eight hours at a time. I had just snuck off to the sleep room near the end of a marathon session when a nurse woke me in a panic.

"We've got a woman in labor who's not progressing," she said, urgency seizing her voice. "The baby's heart rate is variable. We need you now."

After arriving at the labor and delivery area, I found no anesthesiologist, no ob-gyn—just a distressed mother in desperate need for help.

"We've been calling everyone, but no one's answered," said the nurse.

The baby's heart-rate monitor slowed, further alarming the mother and gathering nurses. Worse, the woman still hadn't dilated, and her baby was clearly in distress.

We must do an emergency C-section, I thought. *But I've never done one on my own, let alone without an anesthesiologist.*

The obstetrician arrived, quickly and quietly preparing for surgery. I sighed with relief until I remembered that the anesthesiologist still wasn't here.

"We'll do a conscious sedation," I said, trying to calm the mother.

I opted for a local injection of lidocaine below the umbilicus, the way they did in the old days to make an incision. We opened the abdominal cavity, then the uterus, and finally the amniotic sack to deliver the baby seconds before the anesthesiologist arrived with the pediatrician in tow.

As we resuscitated the baby who was blue, listless, and without a discernable pulse, I was suddenly struck by the moment. Instead of thinking about the success of the resuscitation and the danger lessening by the second with all hands on deck now, I contemplated the anatomy we all share. As the baby was safely placed in the mother's warm embrace, I couldn't help thinking about this protective womb as a model for how we live. For a brief period, we're protected in a controlled environment. We're fed. We're sustained. We grow.

It's a stable, routine-sustaining life, but eventually we must be born. When this happens, our bubble bursts. Out we come, kicking and screaming into a new existence. This pattern repeats throughout our days. It's what we originate from, what we become in our never-ending dance from stability to instability and back again.

This routine constitutes the very essence of life.

* * *

My residency training in psychiatry inspired my interest in human behavior, especially behavior put to the test in stressful environments like the ER story I just told. For more than a decade, I got an up-close peek at the full spectrum of humanity—all its inspiring *and* frightening displays—when I served as associate clinical professor at the Keck School of Medicine of the University of Southern California in the notorious Los Angeles County+USC Medical Center.

However, my frontline experience pales in comparison to the situation the world faced when the COVID-19 pandemic hit in spring 2020. On March 31, CNN reported the Brookdale University Hospital Medical Center in New York reached ICU capacity with patient beds lining hallways of the emergency department and an overflowing morgue. Emergency room physician Dr. Arabia Mollette described the place as a medical war zone. "Every day I come, what I see on a daily basis is pain, despair, suffering, and health-care disparities."

Though hellish, the overwhelmed American health-care system was just a part of the global chaos. Country after country experienced unthinkable tragedies. On March 28 and 29, the United Kingdom "recorded two straight record-high death tolls from the virus, with 944 total deaths in 48 hours," according to *Business Insider*. Within a month, Italy's death toll dwarfed China's. On March 21, the *New York Times* reported, "The government has sent in the army to enforce the lockdown in Lombardy, the northern region at the center of the outbreak, where bodies have piled up in churches. On Friday night, the authorities tightened the nationwide lockdown, closing parks, banning outdoor activities including walking or jogging far from home."

As might be expected, already vulnerable countries endured terrible losses as the COVID-19 whirlwind touched down on suffering populations. According to a March 29 article from *Science*

Magazine, "As of today, Iran has 38,309 confirmed cases and 2,640 deaths—the highest totals in the Middle East. The latest model from scientists at the University of New South Wales predicts that by late June, Iran could see 48 million cases—more than half of its population—without major efforts to curb infections."

In the last few years, war-torn Yemen had already suffered through the world's largest cholera outbreak with more than a million confirmed cases. To avert more deaths from COVID-19, the Secretary-General of the United Nations called for a global ceasefire between pro-government forces and Houthi rebels in March. Unfortunately, this warning went unheeded as violence actually increased with killing in the streets.

Financial fallouts followed on the heels of rising mortality figures in nation after nation. On March 30, *Al Jazeera* predicted massive devastation would disproportionately impact poorer states. "The socioeconomic hit on poor and developing countries will take years to recover from, UNDP said in a report released on Monday, stressing that income losses in those countries are forecast to exceed $220bn. Nearly half of all jobs in Africa could be lost, it also warned."

Meanwhile, business as usual in America stopped being anything close to the definition in March, beginning with athletics, a $500 billion industry. The NCAA canceled the basketball championships known as March Madness. Following suit, the NBA suspended its season until further notice. The PGA tour canceled the Players Championship and all other tournaments until the Masters. Likewise, the NHL paused its 2019–2020 season and Major League Baseball postponed games until May 1, 2020, at the earliest. To retain viewership, ESPN announced it would offer programming of obscure sports most people had not heard of and would most likely never watch except for these unusual circumstances. "Sports such as cherry pit spitting, marble racing, death diving, and sign spinning," according to the *Miami Herald*.

Though streaming services saw viewership numbers spike by a shuttered population hungry for content, overall, the entertainment industry suffered from COVID-19. In March, movie theaters closed, studios laid off staff, film festivals were cancelled, and production schedules stalled. Theme parks, including Disneyland, shut down. According to *Newsweek*, "The industry that thrived during the Great Depression by providing affordable entertainment to a weary nation is experiencing a crisis unlike any other in its history. The effects vary, but all of show business is feeling it."

Backing up to see the big picture, it might be more apt to remove the qualifier in that last sentence to describe what is being called the biggest crisis in mankind's history. At this moment, all of business is feeling it. All of *us* are feeling it. Whether it be elementary, middle school, high school, or college, nearly all classes have gone remote. Commencements have been postponed. Weddings have been canceled. Vast contingents of the economy now work from home (alongside their children). Restaurants have switched to takeout and delivery. And grocery stores have moved to rationing supplies and limiting guests to protect an already stretched supply chain.

These are but a few of the ways the world changed in March 2020 but come nowhere close to describing the full impact. Chronicling the aftermath would require a book—or books—in its own right. This is, of course, beyond our scope. Nonetheless, the above revelations share something in common: disrupted lives. *Stressed* lives.

Even before COVID-19, the 2019 annual Gallup poll found Americans to be "among the most stressed people in the world." When the dust settles from the pandemic, it is all but assured that this number will rise. Prior to coronavirus, escalating internecine and external tensions had whipsawed us all in an era of unmatched volatility. Though the Y2K hysteria at the turn of the millennium proved unwarranted, it's as if the intensity switch never shut off. Coinciding with the rise of the web as "the centerpiece of modern life," and supercharged with the emergence of social media and smartphones, daily experience had already become ever more complex and complicated these last few decades.

Prior to disease updates blowing up our phones, we were being pelted with more content than we could handle. From the second we awoke, a barrage of stimuli and endless demands bombarded us, screaming for attention. *Haven't received the latest push alert?* You must be living under a rock. *Didn't respond to your client's email on Sunday?* You must be a bad businessperson. *Didn't like and share the latest Facebook update?* You must not care about your grandchildren.

We've changed as a result of the ever-present technology mandating more of our attention. Multitasking, for one, has become the new normal. *Want to be successful?* You'd better know how to juggle: work, relationships, a family life. Slip up and the consequences are dire: loss of job, loss of income, loss of security, loss of everything you hold dear. But as COVID-19 has shown, times are changing. *Fast.* And it's time we changed how we respond, too, beginning with how we think.

So Much for Conventional Thinking

For years, we were told that the best way to navigate our noisy new world is to accept change. Open up to novelty. Go with the flow. Live in the moment. Embrace the relentless delivery of content minute by minute. But what if that's wrong? *What if living in a bubble is a good thing?* After all, that's what people the world over were told to do in March 2020.

Social distancing—the act of staying six feet away from others and avoiding crowds—was deemed essential behavior to contain the contagion. But the self-imposed bubble should not only be confined to the physical. Many leading mental health professionals, including Owen Hoffman of Mountain Family Health Centers, have suggested limiting time families spend viewing the news. "As soon as you notice it's making you feel bad, stop watching or tuning in," Hoffman said in an interview for *Post Independent*. "As soon as you start feeling nervous, anxious, depressed, or upset, turn it off and engage in some other useful activity."

This advice makes perfect sense in an age of exploding fear and anxiety. After all, we began life in a bubble, as discussed on page 2. Our nascent experiences can offer us the best road map on how to live now. Consider this: each of us begins life surrounded by a physical membrane. This bubble both nourishes and protects. As fetuses in our semipermeable barrier, we receive amniotic fluid containing nutrients, hormones, and infection-fighting antibodies to ward off diseases. But as we grow older, our bodies continue thwarting outside threats while seeking something called homeostasis. Let us now explore why—and what our bodies can teach us.

What We Seek

Though the technical term homeostasis smacks of boring high school textbooks and Bunsen burners, offered in synonym form it morphs into something more practical sounding: *stability*. Seen again in another synonym, it represents the highest of human ideals: *balance*. Going back to antiquity, Western influential thinkers held balance to be the noblest pursuit of a well-lived life. "Aristotle in particular elaborated the concept in his *Nicomachean Ethics*. The 'golden mean' is the desirable middle between two extremes, one of excess and the other of deficiency," according to *New World Encyclopedia*.

Harmony, yet one more synonym for homeostasis, also guides Eastern philosophical thought. Written by the sixth-century sage Lao Tzu, Taoism's fundamental text, the *Tao Te Ching*, views balance with the natural order to be the apotheosis of a mindful existence. As Lao Tzu writes, "He who is in harmony with the Tao is like a newborn child. Its bones are soft, its muscles are weak, but its grip is powerful. The Master's power is like this. He lets all things come and go effortlessly, without desire. He never expects results; thus, he is never disappointed. He is never disappointed; thus, his spirit never grows old."

Enter Routine

A mother's womb works 24–7 in service of balance. It is forever on call, preventing harmful stimuli from endangering a baby while precipitating its development far from the world's chaos. Yet within this physical bubble lies the first stirrings of a baby's own agency. And what is one of the first things a baby tries to do? Find its own stable way of living. "A baby in the womb will develop their own routine, sometimes very actively, sometimes very still or sleeping and so will not have 'regular movement throughout the day' but will actually have bouts of intense movement and times of quiet—their own daily routine," according to Angela J. Spencer's *Babyopathy*.

At the same time, natural forces cannot help but impact a child's development. Chronobiology, the field of inquiry concerned with how living organisms adapt to solar- and lunar-related phenomena, suggests we humans are wired to respond to cyclic fluctuations. For instance, our bodies wake and sleep at certain times due to unconscious governing rhythms. Interestingly, the term chronobiology derives from the ancient Greek χρόνος (*chrónos*, meaning "time"), and biology, the science of life.

Time itself cannot help but exert its influence on all of us—even in utero. Then, just as soon as we are born, the need for a new bubble begins. Only now, our bubble is no longer just physical. Informed by chronobiology and the uniquely human ability to plan our days, it seems fitting to term this new bubble a *time bubble*. The time bubble consists of those activities and events we select (or are selected for us) to create and maintain a stable environment.

Returning to the first bubble we experience as humans, we can see the time bubble hard at work. Just as a baby born prematurely will often be aided by consistent feedings in the NICU to aid in its development, so does an attentive mother establish regular mealtimes to provide daily structure. She nurtures her offspring not just with physical sustenance, (i.e., milk or formula), but by establishing reliable processes to hasten her child's acclimation to life outside the womb. But what happens next in the life cycle?

Drums Keep Pounding a Rhythm to the Brain

As the beat goes on and Baby develops into Toddler, his or her time bubble increases in intricacy. Parents wishing to provide stability establish routines delineating not just meal and sleep times, but a myriad of activities; hygiene: toothbrushing, bathing, haircuts; wellness: doctor's checkups, vaccines; social: school, playdates, holidays.

As Dr. Laura Markham writes for *Aha Parenting*, "Routines give infants and toddlers a sense of security and stability. They help infants and toddlers feel safe and secure in their environment. Young children gain an understanding of everyday events and procedures and learn what is expected of them as routines make their environment more predictable."

For evidence of the importance of routine on children we may again consider how COVID-19 influenced parental thinking. Across the world, overworked moms and dads returned to the value of schedules to manage disruption to their way of life. To this point, Healthychildren.org suggested establishing a routine to maintain a healthy balance after schools closed. "Since changes in routine can be stressful, it will be helpful to talk with your kids about why they are staying home and what your daily structure will be during this time. Let them help create a daily schedule that can hang on the refrigerator or somewhere they can see it each day. Be sure to include breaks from tele-work or schoolwork to relax and connect with each other."

Returning to the centrality of routine on child development, a physical aspect to the bubble remains ever necessary for toddlers—even in normal times. No longer siloed from the world by the cellular membrane during pregnancy, a little one is now free to roam and explore—to some extent. Even strangers are tolerated so long as they are friendly and trustworthy. Likewise, travel is permitted so long as the child receives the proper precautions, like vaccines. Of course, internal physical processes are still at play. Like all living creatures, every child's body constantly strives for stability to survive. For instance, a host of unconscious key processes regulate temperature, respiration, and digestion.

As the toddler develops, the mental aspect of their time bubble also expands, taking on more importance. Responsibilities increase for the little boy or girl as they age. More is expected. Meaning is added to the routine. As a child grows up, they go to school to learn subjects like history and math. They play sports to develop health and interpersonal skills. They explore art and music to enrich their personalities. They also experience rites of passage, including bar/bat mitzvahs, quinceañeras, confirmations, graduations, and other milestones.

And then the bubble breaks down.

Yale, a Dead French Existentialist, and Our Crisis (of Meaning)

Even before classes went remote across the country, significant developments were occurring at the university level, developments that may be seen as a bellwether for a society in flux. To understand their import, let us set our sights on Yale University. In 2018, psychology professor Laurie Santos introduced what would become the most popular course in the college's three-hundred-year history. Entitled "Psychology and the Good Life," it attracted nearly one-fourth of all undergraduates for a class on . . . *happiness?*

To understand the class's appeal and its raison dêtre, let's get to know its instructor. Forty-two-year-old Santos straddles the generational divide. She can remember life before the web yet is more comfortable with technology than her boomer forebears. Her own history, therefore, made her just the right age—and temperament—to design a class for our times. "When I had a bad day in the 1980s, I might hang out with a friend and complain, take a bath, or do some exercise," she explains in a *GQ* profile. "Nowadays you have this other easy way to feel better or quote, unquote 'feel better' or at least not be bored."

Most of today's young people, when stressed, don't rely on the type of analog remedies Santos mentions in her interview. Instead, many turn to social media for entertainment, answers, and affirmation. But as alarming reports attest, living online can bring untold mental health issues.

Author and motivational speaker Simon Sinek pinpoints dopamine as a source of the problem. Receiving a "like" or "share" can flood our brain with dopamine, the same chemical that makes us feel good when engaging in addictive behaviors. "We have age restrictions on smoking, drinking, and gambling," says Sinek. "But we have no age restrictions on social media and cell phones, which is the equivalent of opening up the liquor cabinet and saying to our teenagers, 'Hey by the way, if this adolescence thing gets you down—help yourself.'"

While it's bad enough that today's youth are consigned to beta test a brave new world unlike previous generations, one in which perceived status is often earned through cyber bullying, deep fakery, and body image manipulation, the core problem runs deeper—all the way to the breakdown of the time bubble. Modern Western culture possesses many positive attributes, but as we will observe in later chapters, it is also suffering from a privation of meaning. Gone are many traditions, rites of passage, and rituals that long ago offered our ancestors stability and purpose.

So, How Did We Get Here?

Once upon a time, rulers and kings used "divine" authority to keep control. People received guidance and direction from religious elders. Priests and rabbis advised us how to comport ourselves based on scriptures. The combined decline of religion and autocratic rule freed mankind in many ways, but it introduced a double-edged sword. Instead of looking outside for guidance on how to live, it forced us to go inward.

The French existentialist Jean-Paul Sartre once said, "Man is condemned to be free; because once thrown into the world, he is responsible for everything he does. It is up to you to give life a meaning." Though our modern culture has yet to put it in these terms, the times we live in require us to make our own time bubble—our own way of dealing with a world in crisis.

A Silver Lining in the Clouds

Let's talk about crisis for a moment. Rahm Emanuel, President Obama's chief of staff once said, "You never want to let a serious crisis go to waste. What I mean by that is it's an opportunity to do things you think you could not do before." Words matter. How we choose to react to events in our lives also matters. We can view COVID-19 and the many other challenges our species will face in the coming years as both real problems and positive opportunities for growth. The trick is shifting our mindset.

Throughout the following pages, I hope to help you see how routine can reframe our thinking. In doing so, we can attain purpose, fulfillment, and joy. Once we understand that we are wired by our physiology and chronobiology to perform routine behaviors, we can transform our thoughts. How? Through *routineology*, the art and science of living one's life through structured and consistent activities. It offers a disruptive idea for a disrupted world: more than just survive, we can thrive by living "in a bubble."

Of course, when people usually say someone is living in a bubble, it's meant to be a bad thing. It connotes being isolated, naive, or possessing a lack of knowledge of the real world. But in our ever-changing environment, living in a bubble takes on new dimensions. It pertains to a search for stability, equilibrium, and a life of meaning. Living in a bubble of our own making can also protect us from chaos while developing our abilities. Returning to the thoughts I had in that hospital room (page 2), we can see how creating and recreating many time bubbles over the course of our lifetime allows us to build stable environments and maintain homeostasis, all the while minimizing stress and improving our chances for survival.

Simply surviving has become the new imperative for people the world over since March Madness in 2020. As soon as the need for social distancing goes down, there will continue to be a need to protect ourselves, but not in a paranoid way. The last thing we want to do is live in a society of fear. After all, feeling stressed only weakens our immune system, making us more susceptible to disease. In light of these qualifications, let it be clear that I am not advocating for a heads-in-the-sand existence, one in which people close themselves off in the name of security.

Instead, I argue we have always flourished when appropriately shielding ourselves for our greater good. The reality is, as biological organisms, our bodies and minds perform well when maintaining an equilibrium. We feel best when our environment is familiar, and our lives possess consistency. Also, by no means am I discounting the importance of novelty. In a later chapter, I go so far as to present the case of a Silicon Valley developer who used technology to introduce randomness into his life. What routineology does show, however, is that seeking balance brings needed structure to our lives in meaningful ways.

Through a mix of compelling behavioral studies, illustrated with insightful and entertaining stories from the worlds of business, sports, and entertainment, you will soon see how creating a time bubble can lead to greater fulfillment, freedom, and joy. Here is just a sampling of stories to come. We will witness how the Rolling Stones have managed to remain the most successful touring rock band after fifty-five years through their own carefully crafted time bubble. We will learn how Thai instructor Nattaporn Lekgerdpong created a routine to protect the morale of his boys during their two-week ordeal trapped in a flooded cave. We will observe how establishing routine protocols can stave off financial crises for today's companies. We will also experience my mother's own story of combating chaos as a prisoner of Auschwitz and how she used routine to live to fight another day—while finding meaning and purpose.

Ultimately, following a routine can ground and guide us. It keeps us accountable to ourselves, ensuring we stay productive and goal oriented. In the following pages, I will also show you how routine doesn't just provide structure to our days, it makes us more successful, and can promote happiness. Most importantly, it can save us when our world turns upside down, when chaos reigns and we don't think we will make it out alive. In the service of longevity, let us now observe how the practice of routine can help us live longer—and better.

CHAPTER 2
A Good Run

IT'S HARD TO IMAGINE just how much the world changed for Elizabeth Sullivan during her lifetime. She was born in 1911, before the invention of television, microwaves, nuclear bombs, helicopters, credit cards, rocket ships, car seat belts—even the penicillin vaccine. Originally from New Mexico, Sullivan witnessed two world wars and subsequent international conflicts in North Korea, Vietnam, Afghanistan, and Iraq. She was actually alive before Russia's last czar was murdered, and his country converted into a communist dictatorship. Of course, Sullivan later saw the Soviet Union collapse. And back when she was just a girl, it was still not legal for women to vote in this country. Elizabeth Sullivan even knew a time in which there were segregated bathrooms for whites and blacks, yet she also lived to see the United States elect its first black president.

By the Numbers

A former math teacher turned diehard baseball fan, Sullivan adored her Rangers—so much so that when the team learned she was turning 106, the mascot captain hand-delivered a cake and gifts to her home in Fort Worth, Texas. Not many people live past the age of 100. Even fewer make it to 106, the year Sullivan passed. According to 2020 data from the United Nations Population Division, the current life expectancy for both sexes (combined) is 73.2 years. Globally, women still live longer. They can expect to reach 75.6 at birth, whereas men can expect to last until 70.8. At present, Hong Kong holds the distinction for the longest life expectancy at a whopping 85.29 for both sexes—a far cry from the dismal projection of 54.36 for individuals living in the Central African Republic.

Even though these statistics are encouraging—at least in comparison to what they were in 1911 when men could only expect to live until 50 and women 53, hitting the 100-year mark is still a big deal. Remember when Willard Scott used to celebrate viewers making it to 100 on the *Today Show*? *Today*'s Al Roker keeps up the tradition because it is still so rare for people to live so long. To understand just how rare, it's helpful to recall the world's population is estimated to be 7.8 billion (according to Worldometer as of 2021). And yet, the United Nations estimates there are only 316,600 living centenarians today.

Observing this stark disparity might lead us to presume folks like Sullivan must live very healthy lives, eating nutrient-rich foods and abstaining from bad habits, like drinking, right? Not Sullivan. Reportedly, she used to drink three cans of her favorite soda daily. "People try to give me coffee for breakfast. Well, I'd rather have a Dr. Pepper," she said in a 2015 interview for WBOC-TV. "Every doctor that sees me says they'll kill you. But they die and I don't, so there must be a mistake somewhere." (Sidenote: Sullivan was known to be so enamored by Dr. Pepper, on her 106th birthday, she received a cake shaped like the can and plenty more cans of soda in a gift basket from Snapple Group, Dr. Pepper's parent company.)

More Anomalies or Something Deeper at Play?

Sullivan's longevity must have been an aberration. After all, what doctor would deign to suggest a nutritional routine composed of intaking sixty-four grams of sugar—three times daily? Maybe Agnes Fenton's. New Jersey's oldest living resident (until 2017) credited much of her staying ability to a daily dose of Miller High Life and Johnnie Walker Blue. According to a NewJersey.com obituary, "Agnes Fenton, who had lived in Englewood since the 1950s, was given the unusual prescription of alcohol by her doctor in 1943 for a benign tumor. She kept it up for decades, before quitting drinking in the last few years as she began to eat less and was restricted to a wheelchair and attended by her nurses."

But Fenton isn't the only centenarian who credited her prolonged duration on a less than nutritious sustenance. According to a 2015 article by Yagan Shah in the *Huffington Post*, ice cream occupied a prime spot in 108-year-old Virginia Davis's nightly routine. Davis informed the *L.A. Times* that every day after eating soup for dinner, she promptly followed it up with a bowl of this Neapolitan treat. "Maybe that's her secret," said the centenarian's caregiver Rebecca Montalban for the *Huffington Post*. "She finishes one gallon in a week."

Astonishingly, the more we observe the routines of other centenarians, the more we witness less than pristine models of behavior. Born in the nineteenth century, Susannah Mushatt Jones held the title as the oldest living person until she passed in 2016 at the age of 116. Her daily breakfast routine included eating greasy food such as eggs, grits, and bacon. "She'll eat bacon all day long," said her aide at the Brooklyn facility where she lived, in an article for *Page Six*.

Along the same lines, consider Fredie Blom. Born in Adelaide, South Africa, a rural town in the Eastern Cape province, Blom is much rarer than centenarians. He occupies an even more elite designation of the elderly. He is a *supercentenarian*, someone who has lived more than 110 years. It is estimated that only 300 such individuals exist in the world at any given moment. Though Blom no longer drinks alcohol and lacks Davis's penchant for ice cream, he possesses his own vice. "Every day I still smoke two to three 'pills,'" Blom told the BBC in an interview. (Pills are slang for tobacco rolled into a small newspaper.)

Contradictory Health Advice Can't Help but Leave Us Confused

Going back decades, Americans have been inundated with conflicting guidelines advising us what to do, what to eat, and what to drink to live longer. "For years, fat was a dirty word in the dietary world. After World War II, large studies established links between saturated fat and heart disease," according to *Harvard Health Publishing*. "[Yet] As it turns out, the 'all fat is bad' message was wrong. Foods that contain fat help fill you up, so you stop eating earlier." Likewise, milk has a storied and contradictory nutritional history. "For decades, the USDA has advised people to consume milk every day," according to *Medical News Today*. "However, some health advocates believe that people do not need to eat dairy to be healthy. Others believe that dairy may even be bad for health if people consume too much of it."

Truth be told, so much of the conventional wisdom concerning how best to live longer has been refuted, revised, and rethought that we can only laugh appreciatively when comedians, like the late Bill Hicks, take to task the prevailing views on how to live longer. In his 1992 comedy show *Relentless*, Hicks contrasted the fate of Jim Fixx, the father of America's fitness revolution, with Yul Brynner, the hard-partying actor who enjoyed a lifetime of excess even into his later years. "Jim Fixx was a health nut who wrote books about jogging and had a heart attack. They should have done a commercial with that guy: 'I'm Jim Fixx. I'm dead now. And I don't know what the f*** happened! I jogged every day, ate nothing but tofu, and I'm dead.'"

Getting to the Truth

Naturally, as a physician I would be remiss to suggest that eating junk food, drinking booze, or smoking is key to a longer life. However, it would be just as inane for me not to draw conclusions from the growing body of evidence suggesting that other (overlooked) factors may be responsible for so many individuals persisting into old age while flouting health prescriptives. Doctors have long been equated with detectives seeking clues. And when trying to understand a mysterious phenomenon, any good sleuth will often look for commonalities between case studies belling a greater truth. *So, what is this greater truth? What is the secret to longevity?*

Warren Buffett, CEO of Berkshire Hathaway, who is pushing 90, recently gave his answer to *Fortune Magazine*. "I checked the actuarial tables and the lowest death rate is among six-year-olds. So, I decided to eat like a six-year-old. It's the safest course I can take." (By the way, Buffett's nutritional routine consists of something straight out of Sullivan's playbook: he reportedly drinks a whopping *five* cans of Coke a day—all while wolfing down copious amounts of ice cream and potato sticks.)

Dick Clark, the radio and TV personality best known for hosting *American Bandstand* from 1957 to 1988, and who lived into his 80s with an eternally youthful appearance, had his own advice for outsmarting actuarial tables. "When I get right down to it . . . I admit I picked my parents very carefully," writes Clark in his book *Looking Great, Staying Young.* "I've been blessed with the good luck of having come from good bloodlines."

Genetics *Does* Play a Role

Glibness aside, strong genetics are a helpful requisite to live longer. According to a study by the NIH's US National Library of Medicine, "The siblings and children (collectively called first-degree relatives) of long-lived individuals are more likely to remain healthy longer and to live to an older age than their peers." While acknowledging that the study of genes' impact on longevity is still a developing science, 25 percent of the variation in human life span is estimated to be determined by genes. However, precisely which genes contribute to a longer life span remains undetermined.

Nonetheless, we have reasons to question the supremacy of genetics on life spans when we consider studies of identical twins separated at birth and raised apart. If genetics was the primary determinant of longevity, each twin should live to be roughly the same age (barring any accident or other environmental consideration). At least that's what Dr. Kaare Christensen, professor of epidemiology at the University of Southern Denmark, hypothesized before conducting an experiment to glean the truth.

Utilizing detailed registries listing all the twins born in Denmark, Finland, and Switzerland from 1870 to 1910, Dr. Christensen and his team isolated their study until it contained 10,251 pairs of same-sex twins, identical or fraternal. Reporting his findings in a 2006 paper published in *Human Genetics*, he found identical twins to be slightly closer in age when they passed than fraternal twins.

Yet even among the identical twins, the majority died *years* apart. This indicates that genes possess a limited influence on how long we live. "Twin studies show that genetic differences account for about a quarter of the variance in adult human lifespan," Dr. Christensen and his coauthors state. "Common polymorphisms that have a modest effect on life span have been identified in one gene, APOE, providing hope that other genetic determinants can be uncovered. However, although variants with substantial beneficial effects have been proposed to exist and several candidates have been put forward, their effects have yet to be confirmed."

To be sure, genetics play a role in longevity, but as Dr. Christensen found and the NIH report confirms, this is but part of the equation. According to the latter: "The duration of human life (longevity) is influenced by genetics, the environment, and lifestyle. Environmental improvements beginning in the 1900s extended the average life span dramatically with significant improvements in the availability of food and clean water, better housing and living conditions, reduced exposure to infectious diseases, and access to medical care."

Now, if we stop to consider the effect of rising standards of living, especially since the end of the nineteenth century when Susannah Mushatt Jones was born, we begin to realize what a difference modern life, with its comforts, convenience, and easy access to food and medicine, has wrought. To drive this idea home, here's Richard Rahn of the Cato Institute, writing for the *Washington Times* on how much better even the poorest live today compared to royalty a few centuries ago:

The average low-income American, who makes $25,000 per year, lives in a home that has air conditioning, a color TV, and a dishwasher, owns an automobile, and eats more calories than he should from an immense variety of food ... [Meanwhile], Louis XIV lived in constant fear of dying from smallpox and many other diseases that are now cured quickly by antibiotics. His palace at Versailles had 700 rooms but no bathrooms (hence he rarely bathed), and no central heating, or air conditioning.

Put in this context, it's not so surprising that the long-persisting individuals detailed in this chapter have endured so long. Though they may have enjoyed some indulgences, they also benefited from a lifetime of stability quite unknown in centuries past.

All Clues Lead to Stability

If we recall from page 7, each organism on this planet is biologically predisposed to seek homeostasis. And what is homeostasis? Writing for the *Scientific American,* emeritus professor Kelvin Rodolfo of the University of Illinois at Chicago's Department of Earth and Environmental Sciences explains it this way: "Homeostasis, from the Greek words for 'same' and 'steady,' refers to any process that living things use to actively maintain fairly stable conditions necessary for survival." In the animal kingdom, the search for homeostasis—or stability—can involve bodily responses to changing environmental circumstances. For instance, dogs pant to reduce their internal temperature when it is hot outside. Likewise, certain rodents have been shown to maintain a constant blood sugar level even when food is in short supply.

As fellow members of the animal kingdom, the importance of stability in our own lives cannot be overstated. It begins with how we are psychologically wired. On page 8, we discussed how each of our time bubbles starts in the womb. Here, aspects of chrono-biology, (i.e., the cyclical rhythms of day and night) impact the sleeping and waking activities of an unborn baby. Once this child enters the world, parental and societal factors affect how its days are ordered. But what we haven't yet discussed is how *instability* can wreak havoc on our psychological development, especially in the early years.

Researchers Heather Sandstrom and Sandra Huerta of the Urban Institute describe such a potential for harm this way in their report, *The Negative Effects of Instability on Child Development: A Research Synthesis*: "To develop to their full potential, children need safe and stable housing, adequate and nutritious food, access to medical care, secure relationships with adult caregivers, nurturing and responsive parenting, and high-quality learning opportunities at home, in childcare settings, and in school."

Knowing how instability can stunt the growth of developing children in so many ways, it's little wonder that a stable environ-ment can so positively impact adults traversing life's various stages. And though experts, especially in the health space, often empha-size the importance of content on longevity such as what we eat, drink, and do, routineology suggests that what matters more is the *regularity* of our lives. Doing things in a consistent fashion—even seemingly negative activities—like smoking, provide our days with a stable time function, leading to a more secure environment in which to pass our lives.

Lighting Up the Dark Corners of Our Existence

To understand why the content of our days is not as important for longevity as doing things regularly to support stability, consider the unknown. Since time immemorial, what we don't know has fright-ened mankind, causing us untold suffering. COVID-19 is a prime example of this. There has never been a more uncertain time in our history. Glimpsing the markets as a sign of the times reveals just how frightened the world is by what we do not know. The stock market crash of 2020 on Monday, March 9, was the largest point plunge for the Dow Jones Industrial Average up to that time. This was followed by two more record-setting point drops on March 12 and March 16.

Setting aside the fears of adults for a moment, children are especially predisposed to fear of the unknown. Just think of darkness and all this void conjures, from monsters to bogeymen. Though parents will often comfort their little ones with reassurances that there is nothing to fear, recent studies have shown this phobia to be evolutionarily rooted. "Humans only really became super predators with the advent of technology, which wasn't that long ago," writes Josh Hrala for *Scientific Alert*. "Before tech, our ancestors were constantly on the look-out for predators that wanted nothing more than to chow down on human sandwiches. To make that even scarier, most of these predators hunted at night—a time of day when we are especially vulnerable to attack because of our relatively poor eyesight."

Of course, fear of the unknown extends to other realms of the human experience. The term xenophobia describes the irrational fear of strange people or situations. Meanwhile, the tongue-twister Metathesiophobia concerns the fear of change. Both phobias concern uncertainty and the feelings of powerlessness it invokes.

Life is full of such moments. After all, entering a room full of strangers can be just as intimidating as receiving an unexpected phone call or not knowing why your car won't start. In a later chapter, we will discuss how artificial intelligence (AI) seeks to mitigate such uncertainty. But for now, let us say, the human psyche has been conditioned to mistrust that which we cannot control or understand to foster feelings of stability. And as we have already seen throughout this book, stability is the ideal condition our bodies and minds seek, whether consciously or unconsciously.

Returning to the fear that kids experience when facing the dark, most any parent is used to soothing their child with reassurances like, "There's nothing under your bed. It's only your imagination." However, we as adults are not always so good at calming our own anxieties when facing the unknown. Not only are we quite aware of actual things to be frightened of, but we also often don't have any protector to turn to for soothing and protection. When we become fearful, we are left to our own devices to regain control over the situation.

With this understanding in mind, let us return to our earlier centenarian examples. The unifying link between these individuals was not their privileged genetics, nor was it even the fact that they liked to engage in vices. Instead, what these individuals shared was a stable environment facilitating a (largely) peaceful transition into old age. They had caretakers invested in their health and well-being. Even if they ate junk food or enjoyed cigarettes, they partook of their indulgences at predetermined times, offering soothing feelings of regularity and consistency. On top of that, each of the examples lived through the twentieth and twenty-first centuries, reaping the benefits of modernity, including access to better housing, nutrition, and medicine.

But What If Things Go Wrong?

Our long-living exemplars demonstrate what's possible when stability reigns. Unfortunately, things don't always go so swimmingly, especially not for seniors, who are particularly vulnerable to life's exigencies. To witness the extent of this problem, we may witness special challenges the elderly faced when confronting COVID-19.

As it's been well-documented in the media, seniors, especially those with heart, lung, and immunological conditions, are disproportionately susceptible to the disease. As *Nature* reported in August 2020, "For every 1,000 people infected with the coronavirus who are under the age of 50, almost none will die. For people in their fifties and early sixties, about five will die—more men than women. The risk then climbs steeply as the years accrue. For every 1,000 people in their mid-seventies or older who are infected, around 116 will die."

The horrific reality of these dire findings correlates with the single largest number of deaths occurring at one place in the United States. In March 2020, *Business Insider* reported more than 60 percent of the country's COVID-19-linked fatalities took place at a Washington state nursing home. "Before the coronavirus hit the Life Care Center in Kirkland, Washington, 120 seniors lived there. Now there are fewer than 50."

Even before the pandemic, the prospect of living in a nursing facility was disconcerting for the elderly and their loved ones for a number of reasons, perhaps the biggest being uncertainty. To understand why, we may look to an article entitled "Why Daily Routine is Important for Seniors: 3 Top Benefits" by *Daily Caring*. "Young or old, people are most afraid of the unknown," the author writes. "As someone loses control over their physical abilities, independence, or cognitive abilities, their world becomes filled with more and more unknowns. And if their days are unstructured and unpredictable, that can add more stress."

Anyone who has ever had to move a loved one to an assisted-care facility is well aware of the toll such instability can inflict on seniors. Coupled with this somewhat normalized fear is the new reality families must face: Will placing my loved one in a senior living center lead to death? In addition to this concern is a new and harrowing challenge for families: by order of health officials, they are not to visit elderly residents for fear of contagion.

So, how will this new mandate affect a population already prone to feelings of loneliness and anxiety? Not well. So far, we have seen that people in their older age require stable environments. Placing them in a nursing home is already bound to elicit feelings of powerlessness and fear, especially as their old way of life—*their old routine*—dismantles before their eyes. This very problem is so pronounced, there is even a term for it: Relocation Stress Syndrome, ". . . characterized by symptoms such as anxiety, confusion, hopelessness, and loneliness. It usually occurs in older adults shortly after moving from a private residence to a nursing home or assisted-living facility," according to the NIH's US National Library of Medicine.

Though there are people, such as Sullivan and the like, who benefitted from a stable environment allowing them to peacefully age, many seniors in facilities today already suffer from a disrupted time bubble. We can predict this problem will only be compounded by COVID-19, especially on baby boomers, a disproportionately massive generation who are entering this vulnerable phase without enough resources to ensure a smooth transition (not to mention, the benefit of being able to see their loved ones on a consistent basis).

Lacking these vital resources, many seniors will undoubtedly suffer from increased stress levels due to their transformed routine, especially those possessing cognitive impairments. Signs of this difficulty may manifest as agitation, confusion, depression, or even despair. Especially among the poor. "Individuals of lower socioeconomic position (SEP) [will] experience a disproportionate burden of stressors that challenge the formation of regular routines," according to the *Gerontologist/Oxford Academic*. Though this is the short-term reality, it's unclear how it will continue, especially if a medication and/or a vaccine is invented to fight the disease.

For now, we can draw comfort from stories such as the following evidencing the power of human endurance.

Despair Not, Going the Distance Is (Well) Within Our Reach

In 2007, Guinness World Records recognized Anthony Mancinelli as the oldest working barber at the age of 96. He held this distinction until 2019 when he passed away. Unlike some other centenarians mentioned in this chapter, Mancinelli didn't live a life of excess. He never heavily drank or smoked. Instead, his was a life of stability centered around his work. After losing Carmella, his beloved wife of seventy years, he found cutting others' hair to be the best way to structure his time bubble.

For fourteen years, he followed the same routine: he would visit her grave every morning before driving himself to his salon in New Windsor. A proponent of stability, he never took daily medication, never wore glasses, and always sought to control his environment. "He [wouldn't] even let anyone sweep up his hair clippings," said his son Bob Mancinelli, 81, in a 2019 article for the *New York Times*. According to Bob, his father even insisted on giving haircuts to himself until the very end.

Stories such as Mancinelli's reveal the importance of intention when it comes to routine. Purposefully and mindfully establishing a consistent order to our lives not only permits us to arrange our affairs more competently, but it also offers us the needed mental space to problem-solve and even dream. Though people often conflate habits with routines, the difference is that the latter is intentional. Or as Jesus Gil Hernandez writes for *Leadership Summaries*, "A habit is an action we do often in a regular and repeated way.

Routine is a regular way of doing things in a particular order. The main difference between habit and routine is that habit is recurrent with little or no conscious thought whereas routine requires a high degree of intention and effort."

Though Mancinelli may have been a man haunted by the loss of the love of his life, he mindfully established a time bubble offering him stability in his final years. As we begin to consider how we might live to his ripe old age, we would do well to emulate his routine.

A related study on just this point by Dan Buettner of *National Geographic* and published in *Inc.* found that people live disproportionately longer lives in five regions of the world: the Barbagia region of Sardinia; Ikaria, Greece; Nicoya Peninsula, Costa Rica; Loma Linda, California; Okinawa, Japan.

Members of this 100+ club, as they are termed, share something in common with Mancinelli. They possess purpose in their lives, giving their days meaning. According to the *Inc.* article, having a sense of purpose can help us live longer. "Reframing your work and life through the lens of purpose brings meaning and fulfillment, and more. Buettner and his team estimate that knowing your purpose, your higher-order reason for getting up and working so hard, can add up to seven years of extra life expectancy."

The Last Word on Lasting Longer

Before closing this chapter, let us reflect on what we have learned. Contrary to prevailing health advice, the content with which we imbue our lives—what we eat, drink, and do—matters not so much for longevity as the act of doing things consistently. More than genetics, which have been shown to have only a 20 percent impact on life span, the activities we engage in affect how long we live.

Pursuing those activities that reduce fear of the unknown and mitigate stress can lead to a more controlled environment, offering stability and aiding in longevity. Coupled with the importance of consistent activities is the need for purpose. As the nineteenth-century existentialist philosopher Friedrich Nietzsche once wrote, "He who has a *why* to live for can bear almost any *how*." As we shall see in the next chapter, the more mindful we can be about living, the better equipped we will be to adapt when our environment suddenly changes.

CHAPTER 3

Wherever You Go, There You Are (Within Your Time Bubble)

"I CHOSE MY PROFESSION primarily for the *lack* of routine," laughs Kim Hester. "I am an adrenaline junkie who gets bored easily, so I picked a job where I get to travel the world solving a myriad of problems and challenges." Hester got her wish working as vice president of sales for JNR Incorporated, where every day is different. JNR is a travel incentive company. For more than forty years, it has been in the business of rewarding top performing employees at large organizations, like Optum Health, with amazing, once-in-a-lifetime experiences in far-flung destinations. "I like to tell people I have been to every place on Earth," says Hester. "*Twice.*"

The travel industry has been severely affected by COVID-19. On April 1, the *New York Times* wrote, "On March 19, the State Department issued a Level 4 'do not travel' advisory, recommending that United States citizens avoid any global travel. This is the highest travel advisory the federal agency can issue. During the same week, the European Union instituted a 30-day ban on non-essential travel to at least 26 European countries from the rest of the world."

Beyond the closing of state borders from Europe to North America, the shuttering of cruise lines, and the huge drop in airline prices, we do not know what travel will look like in the months, let alone years, to come. It remains to be seen if airlines will institute future restrictions. In December 2020, CNN reported, "Now that coronavirus vaccines are starting to roll out in the US and abroad, many people may be dreaming of the day when they can travel, shop, and go to the movies again. But in order to do those activities, you may eventually need something in addition to the vaccine: a vaccine passport application." In the absence of certainty—in a book about managing uncertainty—the best we can do is offer insights on managing a traveling time bubble based on the world we know. (Time will tell if these insights hold true for a post-COVID-19 reality.)

With this caveat in mind, let us return to Hester's experiences as a practiced globe-trotter. Though I have known of the travel incentive industry for years, I am still amazed by the stories Hester tells of the travel programs her organization puts on. "We once arranged for our client to take a group of its top salespeople across a lava field in Iceland to a dormant volcano. When the trek was complete, they got to take a glass elevator seven hundred feet straight down. Here they witnessed absolutely breathtaking rock formations unspoiled by outside contact for thousands of years. It's the kind of unique experience 99.9 percent of the public will never know."

Hester's title, VP of sales, fails to hint at both the extraordinary nature of her profession as evidenced by this story—as well as her considerable duties. For more than a decade, she has been responsible for not just landing the type of elite clientele who can afford to send their best people on safaris where they can sleep under the stars with lions and tigers—she also plans and manages every aspect of these excursions—in person! "My clients call me the 'Wikipedia of Travel' and 'the Travel Whisperer' because I happily share my extensive knowledge and experience of the world with them wherever we go. And though I joke about never wanting a job with a routine, I *do* use many aspects of routine to keep me healthy. And sane."

Before we learn Hester's routines, let's recap. In the last chapter we explored the importance of stability upon longevity. Now we will investigate how to adapt when our environment changes. Travel is perhaps the most common and most significant disruptor of routine. For many of us, the inertia of daily life can breed a time bubble of comfortable reliability. Prearranging our days to our best advantage, we pick the best time to awake and the fastest route to work. Likewise, we carve out schedules to be the most productive while building time for social events and family. We also eat meals and sleep at regular times. And yet this highly structured regimen seems to go out the window the moment we travel.

Why Travel Throws Our Time Bubble for Such a Loop

According to the World Health Organization, "Jet lag is the term used for the symptoms caused by the disruption of the body's internal clock and the approximate 24-hour (circadian) rhythms it controls." Though "jet lag" may conjure up visions of intercontinental travel to exotic locales or the lyrics to Sade's "Smooth Operator" (*Coast to coast/LA to Chicago . . . Across the north and south to Key Largo . . .*), you needn't traverse time zones to upend your time bubble. Just leaving your regular vicinity—for instance, driving to Grandma's—for a long Thanksgiving weekend, can jam up the works.

Why? As previously discussed, humans are subject to the same chronobiological factors affecting every organism on Earth. This means that our bodies and minds react to (often unconscious) environmental patterns, such as sunrise and sunset, as well as subtler changes in light and temperature. Even modern city dwellers living in the shadow of skyscrapers crowding smog-covered skies are influenced by cyclical occurrences of a planet forever in flux.

Circadian rhythms serve as responses to these fluctuations, helping to control each organism's physical, mental, and behavioral changes. To better understand how this works, consider internal timekeeping. The National Institute of General Medical Sciences has found so-called "biological clocks" to be in nearly every bodily tissue and organ. These connect to a master clock. "In vertebrate animals, including humans, the master clock is a group of about 20,000 nerve cells (neurons) that form a structure called the suprachiasmatic nucleus, or SCN. The SCN is located in a part of the brain called the hypothalamus and receives direct input from the eyes." This master clock oversees our activities, syncing our disparate biological clocks, all the while coordinating melatonin production, the hormone responsible for regulating the sleeping/waking cycle.

Though life's continual fluctuations can disrupt *any* organism's internal clock, there is a key difference at play here. Lemurs don't have to frequently change time zones. At least not for business. Only humans do. As a result, we are the only species that suffers from the perils of global travel. Anyone who has flown a transcontinental flight has probably experienced mild physical annoyances, including headaches, insomnia, and irritability. More serious physical effects can include constipation, indigestion, diarrhea, even heartbeat irregularities and increased illness susceptibility.

But what you might not know is that jet lag can manifest in more profound psychological ways. Published in the *British Journal of Psychiatry*, a study found regular fliers through London's busiest airport to be more predisposed to mental illness, including schizophrenia and depression. "In a two-year period, 186 patients were admitted from Heathrow Airport to the nearest psychiatric hospital. Affective illness was related to time zone change."

Meanwhile, in 2017, the BBC reported frequent air travel can lead to higher instances of emotional instability. "An emerging body of research is suggesting that soaring 35,000 ft. (10 km) above the ground inside a sealed metal tube can do strange things to our minds, altering our mood, changing how our senses work and even making us itch more."

As evidence of such emotional disruption, *BBC News* pointed to a survey by Gatwick Airport reporting 15 percent of men and 6 percent of women were more likely to cry watching a film in-flight than at home, prompting one airline to issue emotional health warnings about viewing movies while airborne. "Even lighthearted comedies such as *Bee Movie*, *Bridesmaids*, and *The Simpsons* can trigger the waterworks in passengers who would normally remain dry-eyed if watching these on the ground."

Maintain Your Time Bubble, Even While Traveling

Now that we better understand some of the havoc that travel—especially frequent flying—can cause to both our psyches and bodies, let's turn to Hester's tips on slaying the jet-lag dragon.

Nutrition

"When I am traveling internationally, I stop eating anything with sodium forty-eight hours prior to departure," says Hester. "Sodium makes your feet swell on the plane and generally makes you feel sluggish. Since airline food is *packed* with sodium, I usually bring my own (very fresh) food: salads, fruit, sushi, protein, etc. I also avoid all fried and greasy foods."

Hester has good reason to suggest bringing your own food on board the plane (or at least filling up at the airport food court). A 2019 study by DietDetective.com found that the average airline meal contains more than 800 milligrams of sodium, exceeding the daily limit established by the World Health Organization by a whopping 40 percent.

The Points Guy travel website corroborates Hester's tip in an interview with a seasoned flight attendant. "Eric Foy spends most of his days on planes. So, while you're worrying about the occasional cupcake that your colleague brought to the office, Foy's only option is plane food. That's why he always makes sure to have two things on hand. 'I stick to almonds and water. They help to control your appetite and keep you feeling full longer.'" Foy also recommends paying special attention to hydration. "Lots of times when we are dehydrated, we mistake it for hunger and grab snacks on the plane we could most likely do without. I drink about three liters of water a day to avoid that." Even commercial airline pilots like Mike Burchardi know they need to be careful about what they eat when working. "You really can't have a big steak dinner or a big meal when flying because it can make you groggy. As pilots, we have to be attentive the whole time we're at the helm."

Sleep

"I set my watch to the time zone I am headed twenty-four hours in advance and switch over to the new time with my eating and sleeping patterns," says Hester. "And if I land somewhere in the morning, I never nap during the day. That is the kiss of death when it comes to disrupting your sleep pattern. You won't be able to sleep that night."

Harrison Jacobs concurs with Hester's advice on preemptively adapting one's routine before flying. Another world traveler, he spends sometimes as much as six months on the road serving as international correspondent for *Business Insider*. Prior to departure, he gradually adapts to his intended time zone. "When adjusting my sleep schedule to sleep earlier, I might take a supplement of melatonin, the hormone your body uses to regulate sleep," he writes in a 2018 article. "Or I might restrict my exposure to light by closing the curtains earlier and staying away from phones and screens. If I need to stay up later, I might drink caffeine later than normal, work out late in the day, or just force myself to finish binge-watching that Netflix show."

Like Hester, Jacobs is a proponent of avoiding naps to stave off the jet-lag doldrums. "The worst mistake you can make upon landing in your new time zone is to listen to your body clock." Instead of sleeping—which is what your body wants to do—Jacobs does activities to stay up, like working out or exploring the city. Hester does the same thing. "I power through the day no matter how tired I am. And if I get really sleepy, I take a walk to get some fresh air, then go to bed at a normal time that evening. If you follow this same advice, you, too, will sleep deeply and awake more refreshed and adjusted."

Of course, Hester's and Jacobs's nap abstention mandate is bound to make things harder for travelers who don't sleep well on planes. "Yes, I am one of the fortunate people who can sleep on a red-eye flight. But for those who can't, 5 mg of Ambien for women and 10 mg for larger men will typically put you right to sleep," says Hester. "And since Ambien is a controlled substance, check with your doctor before getting a prescription and never take it more than one to two times per month. It is easy to get so addicted to Ambien (many pilots have this problem) that you can't go without it. Also, I don't recommend drinking alcohol on the plane as it disrupts sleep patterns."

Money

"If you travel a lot, I recommend checking your accounts on a daily basis as part of your routine," says Hester. "The potential for identity theft is high if you use your cards in multiple countries." Though advances in AI for fraud detection have vastly improved, especially in the last decade, it never hurts to take Hester's advice on banking proactively.

A 2018 article in *US News & World Report* by contributor Chris Kissel backs Hester's recommendation. "Even if you don't have any suspicions that your credit card may have been compromised, it's a good idea to keep an eye on your transactions just in case. Also, hold onto your receipts so that you can reconcile your purchases with what you see in your account. If there's something you don't recognize, report it immediately to stop the fraud before it gets worse."

Baggage

"Yes, I also have recommendations when it comes to your packing routine," says Hester. "To stay on the safe side, always carry enough toiletries, make-up, prescriptions/medicines, and clothes in your carry-on to sustain you for one to two days in case your bags get lost." Hester's advice is essential for today's travelers. According to the 2019 SITA Baggage IT Insights report, nearly 25 million bags were mishandled in 2018. This comes despite advancements in radio frequency identification (RFID) technology. It's therefore little wonder Hester advises not leaving packing to chance. After all, accidents happen, and airport purchases can be pricey—if they even have what you need for your trip.

To counteract such difficulties, Hester's packing advice extends to what to wear and what to bring for added stability. "If you are headed to a warm weather destination, pack shorts, tees, and a swimsuit in your carry-on. Also, I never travel without my noise-cancelling headphones, an IPOD, neck pillow, ear plugs, and my own (clean!) soft blanket or pashmina that can keep me warm on planes that are routinely too cold. I also never travel without my Kindle that is loaded with multiple good books in case of delay. Finally, bring a healthy dose of patience on all trips. More often than not, you will need it as delays and misconnects become longer and more frequent."

Finding Stability When Traveling

Now that we have learned from travel expert Kim Hester how best to preserve our time bubble when traveling, I'd like to offer another observation. On page 43, we will explore how establishing a consistent environment—even while traveling internationally—can improve one's performance, whether it be in sports, business, or the arts. Ahead of this discussion, I am reminded of a *Mad Men* episode in which Don Draper, the creative director of a prestigious Madison Avenue advertising firm, pitches a campaign to a fictional patriarch of the renowned Hilton hospitality brand. While flipping through posters of international resorts, Draper asks his client, "How do you say ice water in Italian? *Hilton*. How do you say fresh towels in Farsi? *Hilton*. How do you say hamburger in Japanese? *Hilton*."

In many ways, Draper's pitch foreshadows a marketing tactic that American businesses would come to use when opening up international travel for an emerging global economy, beginning in the 1960s. Seeking to both lure the American traveler abroad—while minimizing their discomfort of the unknown—he strove to have it both ways for his client. "What more do we need than a picture of Athens to get our hearts racing?" Draper asks Hilton point-blank. "And yet the average American experiences a level of luxury that belongs only to kings in most parts of the world. We're not chauvinists, we just have expectations."

Though, of course, Draper never mentioned the term "time bubble" in the hit AMC series, in essence, his marketing campaign sought to streamline travelers' routines by homogenizing their hotel experience. No matter where an itinerant American might go, they could expect to encounter uniform Hilton niceties. Or as Rosie Spinks explains in an article for *Quartz* on this subject, "From hamburgers and milkshakes to air conditioning and tapped-in ice water in each room (an affectation mocked by Europeans), Hilton hotels offered a range of amenities previously unknown in many of the places it opened, even in cities like London."

To this point, in 2017, Swiss photographer Roger Eberhard traveled the world taking pictures of Hilton interiors. What he found was a shocking consistency. According to the *Guardian*: "From Cairo to Cape Town, Paris to Panama, Roger Eberhard crisscrossed the globe photographing Hilton Hotel rooms for his series standard, only to find their décor eerily similar."

Eberhard's pictures reveal the truth of Draper's pitch: the hotel chain knows the value of soothing their customers with the familiar. To maintain a stable environment, one reducing stress and uncertainty, they offer hotel rooms that make their inhabitants feel at home. It would seem that the takeaway for the hospitality sector still applies well into the twenty-first century: the more comfort travelers can expect—*no matter where they roam*—the more enticed they will be to travel outside their comfort zone.

(Not) Working Nine to Five

So far, we have concerned ourselves with how professionals can maintain an optimal time bubble while traveling, but what about those workers whose jobs require them to turn natural circadian rhythms on their heads? To put this situation in perspective, let's turn to an academic paper entitled "Shift Work: Disrupted Circadian Rhythms and Sleep—Implications for Health and Well-Being" published in the NIH's US National Library of Medicine. "Society is increasingly dependent on around-the-clock operations that require shift work," write the authors. "Many industries and services rely on a continuous workforce, including manufacturing, energy production, transportation, health care, law enforcement, and the military."

The paper's study utilized data collected in the United States from 2004 (the most recent year in which such information was comprehensively collected) to develop a composite of the many sectors reliant on individuals working shifts outside the typical nine-to-five workday. "The protective services (police, fire, correction services) have the highest percentage of night and rotating shift workers of any occupation (24.8%), followed by health-care providers (10.9%). Such workers, when assigned night shifts, early morning shifts, or rotating shifts, must modify their sleep schedules from the normal nighttime hours, placing the individuals into a condition of circadian misalignment."

Unsurprisingly, the paper's authors found that prolonged disruptions to the participants' chronobiology led to negative physical consequences, including, but not limited to, increased cancer risks and metabolic imbalances precipitating diabetes. Working anomalous schedules also contributed to deleterious psychological outcomes, impairing numerous facets of life. "Shift work–induced circadian misalignment not only affect[ed] sleep and health, it also determined when people can exercise, eat, socialize, and have sex—all factors that support physical and mental health."

My coauthor, Michael Ashley, experienced these kinds of travails when briefly working a night shift after college. "My best friend and I created a social media company back in 2003. A kind of precursor to Facebook and Craigslist, we called it MUHookitup. com in honor of our alma mater, the University of Missouri. To finance our company and pay our bills, we each got jobs allowing us to keep our days free to meet with potential customers."

In support of this, Michael took a job at an auto parts factory requiring him to work the 12:00 p.m. to 8:00 p.m. shift for three to four days at a time. "The plant had just opened," explains Michael. "To quickly get up to speed, sometimes management would ask us to work sixteen-hour days, often for a whole week."

As might be expected, this routine wreaked havoc in Michael's life. Though he made good overtime money working long hours, the job hurt his ability to meet with clients because it was so physically taxing. "In retrospect, I'm lucky I only worked there for six months. I was twenty-four at the time so I could manage the craziness it imposed, but it definitely wasn't healthy. I feel worse for my coworkers who kept that job and had to deal with that grind for years. I can only imagine the toll it must have taken on their lives."

Nurses are one such group of workers who do manage the strain of shift work for long durations. To better understand how to deal with such chronobiological disruption, we would be well advised to look at how they adapt their time bubbles. "The key to not just surviving but thriving on the night shift is to get adequate rest," writes Winona Suzanne Ball, RN, MHS, for the CNA Plus Academy. "Sleeping well during the day is essential. Just how do you do that?" Ball answers this question by putting forth tips from experienced night staffers.

Ball's most salient tip is to reestablish a routine in which you substitute night stimuli for daytime. She suggests "fooling" the brain by transforming your surrounding environment. "Make your bedroom as dark as possible with room-darkening shades or curtains. Wear a sleep mask to keep your eyes from sensing light; when the brain perceives darkness, it produces melatonin, the sleep hormone. Ear plugs can help by keeping daytime noises out. Some people also like a white noise machine or phone app, which blocks noise with soft moving air."

Though Ball's advice can help those toiling throughout the night as the world sleeps, there is no foolproof solution to manage the difficulties that shift work can inflict. Perhaps the best we can do is try to hack the body's internal clock to reestablish a semblance of stability, even in less than ideal conditions. Doing so is an ideal strategy for restoring the stability of a consistent time bubble.

The Final Frontier

Before concluding this chapter on managing our time bubble despite environmental disruption, let's contemplate the future of travel and how it may affect us from a chronobiological perspective. In 2019, SpaceX CEO Elon Musk made headlines when he announced plans to carry private passengers to the moon in the next few years. His first paying customer was Japanese billionaire Yusaku Maezawa, founder of e-commerce giant Zozo. By 2023 Maezawa plans to bring a group of artists and himself on a round-the-moon mission aboard SpaceX's BFR spaceship rocket combo as part of a creative project entitled #dearMoon to "inspire the dreamer inside all of us."

Meanwhile, Virgin Galactic, founded by billionaire Richard Branson, has already billed itself as "the world's first commercial spaceline" with plans to take up to six passengers into suborbital space for hours at a time to explore the effects of weightlessness (and, of course, marvel at the stunning visuals). As space tourism expands due to these pioneers' efforts and others, it's only inevitable we can expect more ambitious forays into the cosmos. *In the form of space-based weddings?* Yes, indeed. Though this vertical has yet to take off, no pun intended, the Tokyo-based company First Advantage estimated the price tag to be $2.3 million in 2008 when it began taking reservations for couples desiring out-of-this-world nuptials.

However the tourism space industry develops in the following years, one thing is certain. There will be a growing demand to acclimate tomorrow's passengers to a vastly different environment. And undoubtedly, training will encompass physical and mental preparedness. Already, innovative companies are stepping up to fill this niche.

One such organization is NASTAR Center. It has designed a comprehensive program to "provide future space travelers with the core knowledge and skills to become a safe, confident, and capable suborbital spaceflight participant." A Federal Aviation Administration (FAA) third-class medical certificate and a positive physical report are requisites for future travelers. Enrollees who pass this muster can expect to learn how to navigate aerospace, including the particulars of acceleration forces, G protection, and extraordinary physiological and psychological effects.

While companies like NASTAR are acclimating early adopters to extraterrestrial travel, establishing stability in this vastly different environment will remain humanity's future challenge. Just as gutsy explorers once took chances crossing the seas in wooden ships hundreds of years ago, tomorrow's adventurers will be forced to find new ways to reestablish time bubbles ensuring physical and mental stability—or risk deadly consequences.

Richard Garriott de Cayeux is one such individual. The video game developer and entrepreneur reportedly paid $30 million to Russia's Space Adventures to spend twelve days aboard the International Space Station. He reports enjoying the remarkable lifetime experience, but admits he had to ready himself way ahead of time. According to *Star Tribune*, "His time in space required a year of difficult preparation. 'If you're going on a spacewalk, you need to be in excellent physical condition, because an inflated space suit is hard to bend. But if you're not, you just need to be healthy.'"

Unlike Marco Polo or Christopher Columbus, Cayeux benefited from modern medical technology, including intense physical testing. "In my case, they found I was missing a vein on one lobe of my liver," says de Cayeux. "On Earth that's irrelevant, but in space, it could have led to internal bleeding, which is why I ended up having surgery to remove that lobe."

Ultimately, however, the real training involved mental preparation. Cayeux had to develop ways to keep his psychological outlook stable enough to weather any challenge he and his crew might face. Or as he explains, "You need to make sure that the people on the vehicle are . . . serious, confident, positive, and will work to address situations that come up. Every person has a psychologist assigned to them, from Day 1 until launch, to make sure they'll be a safe crew member."

Though our nascent forays into space demonstrate our abilities as a species to transcend our environment, they also serve as a reminder that no matter how far we go—even into the cosmos— we are still constricted by chronobiological forces compelling us to seek homeostasis. Even if we end up colonizing the moon, Mars, or some other planet, we are bound by environmental constraints. To counter these, and better yet, thrive in untold ways, we must establish new routines infusing our lives with stability and purpose. This latter element is important when it comes to our next chapter's theme: how to keep it together—even when everything is falling apart.

CHAPTER 4
When the Walls Come Crashing Down

"YOU DON'T GO INTO COMBAT thinking you'll ever be shot down or become a prisoner of war," says Charlie Plumb. "You couldn't do your job if you felt like you weren't gonna make it. 'Course, I never thought the Vietnamese had a gun big enough to shoot down Charlie Plumb!"

The Unexpected Occurs

A farm kid from Kansas, Charlie Plumb grew up with big visions of flying airplanes, but never thought he would get his chance. Then the Vietnam War escalated and suddenly Uncle Sam came calling for pilots. Plumb couldn't enlist fast enough. Fresh from the naval academy, he completed flight training before reporting to San Diego's Marine Corps Air Station Miramar. Here, he cut his teeth piloting the first adversarial flights of what would later be called TOPGUN. The next year, Plumb's squadron, the Aardvarks, took off from aircraft carrier USS *Kitty Hawk* with fighter squadron 114. Code named "Plumber," Charlie Plumb flew seventy-four combat missions over North Vietnam in the F-4 Phantom jet, successfully executing more than one hundred carrier landings.

But then five days before the end of his tour—Plumb's luck changed. His seventy-fifth mission began innocuously enough before dawn on May 19, 1967. Before midmorning he soared above the clouds toward enemy targets. "I was at the top of my game," says Plumb. "At age twenty-four, I was high on life, flying the hottest airplane in the world. I also had a beautiful wife back home whom I was about to go to see."

Plumb felt the surface-to-air missile slam into him before he heard it. The twelve-thousand pounds of jet fuel on board exploded at the same time his instruments panel lit up like a Christmas tree. Red lights blinked crazily as everything failed. Then, Plumb lost control of his F-4 Phantom as it careened into a dangerous topsy-turvy spin.

Plumb and his radar intercept officer in the two-seater jet had no choice but to eject. Ninety seconds later, they came down in a rice paddy. Armed civilians captured them immediately, blindfolding and gagging them. After being beaten, Plumb and his crew member were moved to a village where uniformed soldiers took him to what would be the first of several prisons he would call home.

Stuck in That Hanoi Pit of Hell

It's hard to qualitatively explain the suffering Plumb endured so I will attempt it in numbers. Plumb would come to spend 2,103 days (5.76 years) in an 8' x 8' cell as a prisoner of war (POW). He could walk only three steps before hitting a wall. There were zero TVs, zero books, zero paper, zero pencils in his cage. He received two small bowls of rice a day and boiled water to drink. One two-gallon bucket served as his toilet. One tin roof often served as an oven, baking him in his cell. In addition to daily beatings (too numerous to count), he lost track of his tears as he sweated and bled through endless days at starvation's edge. At one point, so many boils covered Plumb's depleted body, it caused his eyes to swell nearly shut.

Shot in the Dark

Plumb's prison camp, infamously dubbed the Hanoi Hilton, was located in downtown Hanoi, a heavily defended city. Eager to get inside and take out some of the enemy's power plants and factories, the US flew numerous missions into the capital, shelling nearby targets. One day, a 50-caliber shell from one of those missions came crashing through the roof of Plumb's cell.

It was an armor piercing tracer, but Plumb knew it to be the result of a random shot because US forces weren't trying to strafe his camp. At the time, Plumb was under his bed (a wooden door on two sawhorses.) He watched in wonder as the shell bounced before making a dent in the stucco wall.

But Plumb was even more interested in the damage above him.

"The shot had made a little hole the size of my thumb in the corrugated tin roof. Prior to this, it was always dark in my cell. We had no windows or doors. No way to see out. Only now when the sun came up, it would cast a little beam of light on my floor . . ."

* * *

Born in Vienna on March 26, 1905, Viktor Frankl was interested in the workings of the mind from an early age. As a teen, he did so well in his studies, including a course on Freudian psychological theories, he contacted the man himself to discuss his ideas. Reportedly, Freud was so taken by young Frankl's paper that he took the liberty of publishing it in the *International Journal of Psychoanalysis*. Successes like these, along with receiving his medical degree in 1930, led Frankl to spearhead a neurology and psychiatry clinic in Vienna.

But then his luck changed too.

Adolph Hitler came to power in Germany, initiating a terror campaign throughout Europe. Frankl and his loved ones were caught up in a sweep as SS soldiers sent Jews and other minorities to their deaths at concentration camps, such as the dreaded Auschwitz. In the years to come, Frankl would come to lose everything he held dear in the world: his mother, father, brother—even his pregnant wife. He lost them all to the butchery of the Nazi regime.

And yet, Frankl refused to part with one thing—that which makes us human. Or as he says, "Everything can be taken from a man but one thing: the last of the human freedoms—to choose one's attitude in any given set of circumstances, to choose one's own way."

* * *

This brings us back to Plumb's story. The recent arrival of a 50-caliber shell had torn a hole in his roof, permitting sunlight to pierce the darkness. In the days to come, Plumb would use this intervention to devise the routine that would save his life.

Counting Days

It all began with Plumb tracing the concrete floor with a broken brick as a beam of sunlight made its daily journey across his cell floor. He used the sunlight's path to concoct a means for measuring time.

"I figured out the apogee of the arc, allowing me to pinpoint high noon," says Plumb. "Then I marked off what I thought would be hours. Of course, this was a rough guess, but I had made myself a clock! I also had something of a calendar, too, by tracking the sun's changing position. Depending on things like how high the little speck of light would rise or fall, I learned to predict seasons."

This breakthrough gave Plumb resources to develop his time bubble. It may sound like a minor development, but this event speaks to Frankl's point. A little crack of light opened something deeper in Plumb's psyche. It freed him to choose an attitude of perseverance, defying his circumstances.

"I could now organize my day," says Plumb. "When I figured it was eight o'clock in the morning, I would start my exercise routine. The first meal came at what I figured to be ten o'clock and the second meal arrived about two o'clock. So, after the second meal, usually when the guards were taking their siesta, this was my time to be with my wife."

For the next hour, Plumb would imagine in detail the day he would be freed and return to the love of his life. Relying on his imagination, he conjured detailed mental images of future Christmases, replete with Douglas fir tree branches weighed down by ornaments, honey-baked hams roasting in the oven, snow-covered lawns perfect for building snowmen, toasty cups of hot chocolate with whipped cream and marshmallows, and presents galore for all of the children he and his wife would have just as soon as he got the hell out of Hanoi.

Meaning in the Darkness

Of course, Plumb thought about escape. A lot. But this was years before the movie *The Deer Hunter,* and nobody was successfully escaping from organized prison camps in Vietnam, so instead, Plumb put his efforts into getting by. Following a strict physical routine, he exercised daily to stay fit. Despite deplorable hygiene conditions, he managed to stay clean, avoiding sickness.

Most importantly, he worked on keeping his mind healthy. In addition to dreaming about how he would one day spend time with his wife and an eventual family, in the evenings, he invented "showtime." For an hour, he recalled every movie he had ever seen. To keep his sanity, he would go through them all in his imagination, scene by scene, line by line, actor by actor.

"Life *is* a choice—a choice every day," says Plumb. "You can become the victim, or you can become the victor." We can see this truth today in stories of hope and inspiration in the wake of the COVID-19 virus. For instance, after suffering devastating losses of life, the entire country of Italy went on lockdown, shuttering businesses and emptying piazzas. And yet according to Erica Firpo writing for BBC, there was still hope. She describes looking out her balcony and seeing flags flying the words *andrà tutto bene* (everything will be alright). Meanwhile, she and her fellow citizens found novel ways to connect:

> Every day, as the bells chime 18:00 in our Roman neighborhood, we open our windows and sing uplifting Italian classics with our neighbors. Yesterday, it was Nino Manfredi's *Tanto pe' Cantà* (Just for singing); today, it's Al Bano and Romina Power's *Felicità* (Happiness); and tomorrow it'll be Rino Gaetano's *Ma il cielo è sempre più blu* (The sky is always bluer). We turn up the volume, dance at the window, and wave to our neighbors across the piazza. In just two weeks, this 18:00 tradition has become fundamental to our daily

routine and spread across Italy, becoming the country's new national pastime to spread hope and boost morale.

Though Plumb saw men succumb to victimhood, he also witnessed similar acts of touching humanity. As the sweat-soaked days ticked by, enumerated by his beam of sunlight, Plumb witnessed life-affirming displays of the quiet dignity Dr. Frankl describes in *Man's Search for Meaning*, his own account of survival from unspeakable abuse at the hands of his Nazi captors.

Plumb became close with his fellow inmates also hurting in the dark, including a young naval aviator named John McCain who arrived in worse condition than most with numerous broken bones. Together, their lives plodded on in obscurity, each a Rip Van Winkle, oblivious to outside events, like the assassinations of Martin Luther King Jr. and Bobby Kennedy, riots at Kent State and the Democratic convention, Woodstock, the moon landing, and so on. Far from such developments, Plumb's prison became his whole world with his fellow inmates at the center.

Unfortunately, these men were forbidden from openly talking, especially from cell to cell. Still, they knew they must find a way to communicate to survive. "Let me put it this way," says Plumb. "If a guy was put in that camp that couldn't connect to someone else, he probably wasn't going to make it. That's why we made connection such a high priority. Anytime a new man came into the camp, it was the first thing that happened. Get him communication, teach him the code, bring him around."

The code Plumb is referring to is a complex system of messaging the men devised. It consisted of taps on a wall or tugs on a wire through a hole near the floor. Letter by painstaking letter, this is how the prisoners communicated through their thick walls. For years.

Survival Became His Purpose

In the military, you never have to question your purpose, according to Plumb. If you somehow didn't know it, you asked your drill instructor. He'd tell you in no uncertain terms what it was. But in the hands of the enemy, Plumb's purpose became singular: to get out alive. "Survival became our main purpose," says Plumb. "Our be-all, end-all. That's why routine loomed so large. Planning the future—*dreaming a future was even possible*—gave me and the others a sense of purpose."

Despite such conditions, Plumb made lasting friendships, further fueling his sense of purpose. Whenever he had the opportunity to speak to his roommate, he would go through his life story, beginning with the small town in Kansas where he grew up. "You end up telling the other guy every book you ever read, every girlfriend you ever had. And, then if you transfer camps and you're with a new roommate, you start over again. You tell your life story *and* the life story of your old roommate."

* * *

In this way, Plumb managed to survive nearly six years in his 8' x 8' cell until March 1973 when he and nearly 600 other POWs were allowed to go home at last, their release negotiated as part of the Paris Peace Accords. Before weaving Plumb's story into the bigger picture, let's recap. So far, we have seen how the practice of routine begins in utero with our first bubble, the womb, and how young children come to follow time bubbles as their world expands. Arranged by parents or caretakers, these time bubbles contain the activities that don't just fill our days but provide us with an identity as we develop.

But good routines don't just ground our lives with structure—or stability aiding in longevity—they can actually save us when our world turns upside down. As Plumb's story demonstrates, the importance of our perceived sense of agency cannot be overstated. Plumb was floundering, both physically and mentally, before he found a way to reassert control over his surroundings. Not until he found that speck of sunlight did a glimmer of hope emerge.

Why? As we have seen, humans are wired to survive by seeking out stable environments allowing us to thrive. Driven by the human need to create a stable environment, Plumb came to produce a new mode of existence governed by the reliability of time. Prior to this development, he was literally in the dark. However, the arrival of sunlight allowed him to structure his days, easing his psychological state.

Choice as a Vehicle for Feelings of Control

To understand why this small event should matter so much to Plumb's psyche, let's consider an academic paper published in 2010 in *Trends in Cognitive Science* entitled "Born to Choose: The Origins and Value of the Need for Control." The authors write, "Just as we respond to physiological needs (e.g., hunger) with specific behaviors (i.e., food consumption), we may fill a fundamental psychological need by exercising choice. While eating is undoubtedly necessary for survival, we argue that exercising control may be critical for an individual to thrive. Thus, we propose that exercising choice and the need for control—much like eating and hunger—are biologically motivated." What this means is that in the same way humans come to rely on nutrition to physically sustain our bodies, our minds require choice for mental sustenance. On the other hand, suffering such privation is akin to suffering psychological starvation.

Overcoming Invisible Shackles

To understand how lack of choices can be just as harmful to the mind as lack of food to the body, meet Shujaa Graham, who spent three years in solitary on death row after being framed for murder. Talk about lack of choices. Most of us can scarcely imagine something so limiting.

An article, "What It's Like Living on Death Row," by columnist April Taylor's *Ranker* helps put such dearth in context. "Everything is restricted, including how frequently prisoners can shower. Between showering, exercise, routine checks, and the occasional visitor, death row inmates receive an average of one hour out of their cell per day. Unless they're in their cell, showering, or in the prison exercise yard, they always have handcuffs on. Therefore, any approved visitation time is accompanied by being cuffed the entire time."

Clearly, being on death row is no walk in the park. But it's got to be worse for someone who shouldn't be there at all like Graham. Born in the South, he grew up on a segregated plantation before moving to California, where he experienced race riots and police hostilities. As a youth, Graham bounced between juvenile institutions before landing in Soledad Prison at the age of eighteen. Here, within the prison walls, he learned to read and write, studying history and world affairs. But then he was framed for murdering a guard at the Deuel Vocational Institute in Stockton and sent to San Quentin's death row.

A growing number of experts suggest solitary confinement of the type Graham endured to be more torturous than capital punishment. In light of COVID-19, most of us know only too well the toll that isolation can take on a person. Sharon Salt, senior editor for *Neuro Central* explains the havoc it can wreak on the mind:

Some people will have a support system around them including friends, family, and pets, whereas others will be more alone. The latter can feel very surreal, as the feelings of loneliness and isolation can be heightened. For individuals who struggle with mental health issues this can be a scary situation as they are likely to struggle more during this time and feel more isolated. Thus, people with mental illnesses may experience worsened symptoms from self-isolation but also, it could spark the onset of mental health issues for individuals who haven't encountered them before.

Physician and journalist Atul Gawande is very familiar with such feelings. As he writes in the *New Yorker*, "Solitary isn't just lonely. Those who spend extended periods in isolation often start to lose their minds. Simply to exist as a normal human being requires interaction with people."

Craig Haney, a social psychologist at the University of California, Santa Cruz, concurs. The author of a 2018 article on this subject in *Annual Review of Criminology*, Cruz describes solitary confinement's negative effects this way:

People suffer in these environments, experiencing a range of what can be severe, negative psychological effects, including forms of depression and hopelessness. People experience anxiety attacks. They feel as if they're on the verge of a breakdown. I've had prisoners tell me they spend countless hours worried about whether they're going to be able to come out of this with their sanity intact. Frankly, some of them are unable to. Some people lose their grip on reality.

Graham was not going to be one of those people that snapped. "I kept myself occupied," he said in an interview for *Business Insider*. "I programmed myself." Similar to Plumb, Graham consciously developed a time bubble to structure the content of his days. Every day he woke at 5:00 a.m. and performed exercises, like jumping jacks and push-ups. After sponging himself off in his sink, he would later go into a deep meditative state, pretending to visit his mom and other family members for hours.

Heroes, Not Victims of Circumstance

There are important parallels between Graham's predicament and Plumb's, ones aligning with Albert Camus's allegory in *The Myth of Sisyphus*. In Camus's fable, Sisyphus is condemned for eternity for betraying Zeus. The terms of his punishment are that he is to repeatedly roll a boulder up a hill every single day—only to see it roll right back down again. Zeus believed his punishment to be soul-crushing. So much endless effort—day in, day out, for naught—was bound to drown Sisyphus in the horrible futility of his exertions.

But that's not the point of the essay. Instead, Camus views Sisyphus's struggle as a *triumph* by taking a different viewpoint. By knowingly facing his punishment with honor, Sisyphus defies his tormentor. Instead of choosing to view his sentence as a bad thing, he regains the upper hand by witnessing the power of agency. Though Zeus decreed Sisyphus must do this thing every day, Sisyphus alone gets to choose *how* he will do it; for instance, how he will roll the boulder, how many steps he will take, what he shall think and do as he carries out his "punishment."

In a nutshell, Sisyphus's situation exemplifies the absurdity of life and its beauty, according to Camus. Yes, we don't get to choose our circumstances; but we *can* decide how to face them and, in the process, become heroes, not victims. As Camus writes, "I leave Sisyphus at the foot of the mountain! One always finds one's burden again. But Sisyphus teaches the higher fidelity that negates the gods and raises rocks. He too concludes that all is well."

Like Plumb, Graham didn't have much choice about where he ended up. However, once there, he could choose how to face his circumstances. He could *negate the gods and raise rocks*. Both men did just that. Despite overwhelming odds, they created time bubbles demonstrating their humanity. They also found physical outlets to sustain their bodies while engaging in mental pursuits for purpose.

One final note: Graham eventually won his freedom in 1979 when the California Supreme Court overturned his death sentence because the district attorney had excluded all African American jurors from his trial. Yet, Graham still didn't see the light of day until 1981, when he was finally found innocent and released.

Changing the Within to Manage the Without

One more story demonstrates a Sisyphean struggle between people and their fate. On June 23, 2018, twelve boys talked their twenty-five-year-old assistant coach Ekapol Chanthawong into letting them explore Thailand's vast Tham Luang cave system after soccer practice. According to Chanthawong, they had no food and only planned to stay for an hour. They needed to return before nightfall since one boy had to get back for his private tutor lesson and another had a birthday party celebration.

However, by the time the group arrived at the cave, water from seasonal monsoon rains had already begun pooling beyond the mouth. Still, they decided to venture on. Before they realized just how late it had gotten, they received the shock of their lives: floodwaters had blocked their exit. They were trapped.

Chanthawong and the boys were stranded without food, sealed away in the darkness from everyone they had ever known. "When we are no longer able to change a situation, we are challenged to change ourselves," Dr. Frankl once said. Forced with facing reality, the one thing we have control over is our reaction, according to Frankl. Taking this idea further, creating or following a routine during times of crisis doesn't just give us something to do, it also infuses our lives with purpose and meaning.

Just ask Chanthawong. Soon after realizing they were stranded, the group leader created a routine for the boys to follow that allowed them to keep their wits throughout the ordeal. He also assigned them activities to keep up their spirits. As Panaporn Wutwanich and Shibani Mahtani write for the *Washington Post*, "Faced with a group of hungry, weakening boys, Ekapol urged them to drink water to keep full and to try to dig holes out through the cave with rocks, so that they had a sense of purpose. With a routine of digging, water breaks, and meditation, a group of young Thai soccer players and their coach stayed alive while trapped in a flooded cave without any food for nine days before they were found by two British divers."

Work Purpose Will Set You Free

Along the same lines of Chanthawong's keeping his players busy to provide them with purpose, my mother once found a productive outlet to help her, too, survive an unspeakable ordeal. Back then, her name was Eva Gold, and she came from a small town in Romania. She was young, adventurous, and eager to attend fashion school.

She had no idea that what she learned there would one day save her life.

At this time in the early 1940s, there was a tremendous amount of organization involved in education. Those studying design, like my mom, also learned the use of sheers and measurement, as well as the intricacies of the sewing machine. Like how an army private might acquire the nuances of cleaning and assembling a rifle, she became familiar with her sewing machine. Each day she would ensure the wiring was intact and working properly. She became adept at taking apart and cleaning the tension assemblies. Likewise, she knew how to replace the bobbin winder spring and understood how the foot controller connected to the overall device.

When the Nazis invaded Hungary, she and her sisters were placed in a cattle train to Auschwitz. Upon arrival, they had to strip and be disinfected and examined. My mother and her four sisters were all together when Dr. Mengele (the Angel of Death, as he would come to be known) arrived to inspect. He strolled down the line of nude women, deciding in a split-second who would live and who would die. My mother tensed as he passed, worried he might sentence her due to her slight scoliosis. He paused to look at her carefully for a full second before allowing her to join her sisters in the line to work—and live.

"Work will set you free," read the words at the entrance to Auschwitz. They couldn't be truer. The ability to do something meaningful allowed inmates to survive. (Not just in the psychological sense that Frankl meant, but in a real, physical way. Anyone who didn't work was sent to the gas chambers or shot.)

Soon after arrival, my mother heard a woman ask, "Who can sew?"

My mother raised her hand.

The woman said, "Hmmm. Let's see if you really can. Take apart this sewing machine and put it back together."

Everyone, including the SS officers, turned to look at my mother. If she couldn't be useful at the camp, there was no reason for her to live.

Fortunately, she could do as asked since it had been a part of her routine for so long. Her skill set was noticed. The guards made her a seamstress and assigned her to mend the clothes of those who perished in the gas chamber. Thereafter, promptly at noon on Saturdays, SS officers would arrive to collect their wives in the latest outfits to go to the cinema, concerts, or dinner parties. Along with the other seamstresses, my mother was allowed to live to ensure the wives of the officers had beautiful clothes to wear. However, the real reason I believe she survived when so many others didn't—including other seamstresses—was because she found quiet purpose and meaning in her days, awful as they were.

Though it's easy for us to look back on this period and think that the people at the camps merely had to hang on for a few more days and they would be fine—that's not at all what the prisoners must have thought. People like my mother had no idea how long their ordeal would last. Just like Charlie Plumb, Shujaa Graham, Ekapol Chanthawong, she was in the dark—left to her own devices to survive.

And like these other heroic examples, my mother found the courage to live by changing within to suit her circumstances. Something as trivial as sewing a button correctly became a life-and-death activity for her. Ultimately, she rose above her misery because she derived meaning from the activities of her new routine at Auschwitz. In doing so, she also found the purpose to go on.

Now that we have seen how routine can aid individuals in their darkest hour, in the next chapter we will observe how groups can benefit from observing rituals in the service of stability and certainty.

CHAPTER 5

Is It Time to Bring Rituals Back?

ACCORDING TO LEGEND, the Mesopotamian deity Marduk led the charge of new gods in an epic campaign against the old. Triumphant in his siege, Marduk rose to supreme prominence. He ruled over all other gods and was associated with justice, compassion, healing, magic, and, yes, even fairness—despite sometimes being known as the "Storm God."

After defeating his enemies, Marduk created the sky and earth, as well as the first humans, becoming the patron god of Babylon. Marduk also decreed thereafter that people would do the work he and his god compatriots had no time for. In return the gods would care for them.

* * *

Myths like the above provide identity and enforce group stability. And as we have seen throughout this book, all organisms are wired to seek just this. However, what differentiates us from other species is that we also seek meaning and purpose. In the last chapter, we witnessed the truth of Nietzsche's quote, "He who has a *why* to live for can bear almost any *how*." Through stories of struggle, including my mother's ordeal at Auschwitz, we observed how individuals can reassert dominion over their circumstances by establishing routines that not only order the *how* of their days, but also provide the *why*. Now let's expand our discussion from the individual's search for meaning to the group.

To do so, let us turn our attention to Joseph Campbell, the celebrated mythologist who published *The Hero with a Thousand Faces* in 1949. He once said, "Myths are public dreams, dreams are private myths." Just as personal routines transform into group rituals, the best myths and rituals tend to go hand in hand, providing groups with purpose and meaning.

To better understand this truth, let us return to the Mesopotamian people. For generations, myths, such as the above about Marduk, served as basis for rituals ordering their lives. What's more, myths offered the group answers to life's many questions. Their origin story provided a cosmological explanation and a rationale as to why they were created. Myths like these also offer a counterpart to ritual. The more a myth is repeated, the more it grows in importance, offering the group an identity and à raison dêtre. Perhaps, most important of all, rituals and myths offer certainty in a world teeming with uncertainty; they teach us how to live—and how to die.

A Coordinated Sequence of Actions Makes All the Difference

Before delving into how myths support cultural identities, let's investigate the concept of rituals. Why do formalized activities affect us so profoundly? Zach Laurie, founder of Roots to Branches LLC, has an answer. "Rituals represent an honoring of milestones in our lives and a reorientation of our human existence from a broader lens." As evidence for this, he points to the ancient Greek concepts of *Chronos* versus *Kairos* concerning time. Chronological (Chronos) or linear time is our typical mode of living. We react to things on a moment-to-moment basis. "Observing rituals, on the other hand, allows us to enter into non-linear (Kairos) time to see the 'bigger picture' above our individual (and admittedly smaller) ego-based perspective."

But rituals serve other key purposes, too. They celebrate collective beliefs (such as a nature-based solstice gathering or a cultural event, like Yom Kippur). They can also demarcate a period of transition from one phase of life to the next. Laurie is well acquainted with such transitions. He formed Roots to Branches LLC in 2013 in Marin County, California, to help young people enter adulthood via rites of passage with the guidance of cultural elders and in the context of current societal and educational structures. He did so because he was concerned about the dwindling of such experiences in modern culture. "Devoid of regular milestone celebrations demarcated by ritual, we are collectively ignoring the importance of individual and community development in a cultural and natural context," he says. "When this happens to a person, it can stunt their development, making them unwilling to enter into new life stages with increased responsibility."

We can observe this trend in the form of extended adolescence as popularized by psychologist Erik Erikson. He labeled this stage "psychosocial moratorium," a period in which young adults idle in a hiatus between childhood and adulthood. Instead of entering the job market, marrying, and/or settling down, people in their twenties today are more inclined to live with their parents, play video games, and casually date. Though sociologists have coined them the "boomerang generation" because economic forces have driven them to reside longer with their folks, something deeper may be at play here. "Not only are many young people blocked from reaching adulthood, but they are bombarded with role models for childish and irresponsible behavior," writes Stephen Schwartz, PhD, in *Psychology Today.* "Lifestyles that would have been considered deviant 50 years ago are now commonplace."

The lifestyles Schwartz refers to are the logical outgrowth of a culture lacking meaningful rituals, according to Laurie. "When collective ritual become sidelined by consumerism and replaced by large-scale sporting events (possibly the only current collective ritual besides organized religion), we see traditional healthy community values of cooperation and non-violent communication supplanted by competition and dogmatic polarizing ideas (win versus lose)."

One way to reverse the alarming trend Laurie describes would be to place added importance on rites of passage in our culture. Though some families and communities celebrate milestone events, like bar/bat mitzvahs and quinceañeras, only a small proportion of the public participates in them and they are often viewed as a more expensive version of children's birthday parties.

However, it wasn't always this way. Throughout history, examples abound of communities celebrating developmental stages, such as menstruation or the appearance of pubic hair, in which the group acknowledged an individual's progression through life. Arnold Van Gennep keyed in on this. The anthropologist was the first to coin the concept and term "rite of passage" in his 1909 book *Les Rites de Passage (The Rites of Passage).* According to the *Encyclopedia of Psychology and Religion,* "Van Gennep's basic premise was that there are universal, seminal points in peoples' lives that mark significant transitions in life and are celebrated through cere-monies and rituals that cement these processes and growth within the initiate's community. He was the first scholar to see the overlap between the religious rituals involved and psychological aspects affected."

Rites of Passage 2.0?

To bring needed stability and group cohesion to a modern cul-ture that no longer observes such rituals en masse, it's helpful to recall how seminal events, like a vision quest, once benefitted the collective. Those unfamiliar with this term may still recall the 1985 movie of the same name in which Louden Swain (Matthew Modine) struggles to find meaning and purpose in life upon turn-ing eighteen. Against his dad's wishes, he vows to go it alone and take on the defending state wrestling champion.

Though somewhat informed by the Native American tradition, this Hollywood movie is a far cry from the actual vision quests so often observed in this country before the appearance of European settlers. Though each ritual might vary according to tribe, the basic premise goes something like this: a clan would place a young boy in a remote area by himself. Armed with little but his wits to sur-vive, he would be forced to develop resilience as well as faculties that would one day serve his tribe.

As TokenRock.com explains further, "The seeker finds a place that is special to them and creates a ten-foot circle in which to spend the next two to four days fasting in solitude. A vision usually comes in the form of what Native Americans call an animal totem. These animals can appear in a vision or be a physical representa-tion. Each animal totem has a message that will help guide the seeker in their journey." The beauty of such a ritual is that when the young man returns to the group, he arrives with a clearer sense of purpose and a better understanding of his abilities. Informed by his vision, he knows his intended role in the collective (whether it be hunter, boat maker, medicine man, etc.) and sets to work, transforming his vision into reality for the benefit of all.

While it's not practical—nor needed—for every child to undergo such an arduous undertaking nowadays to understand their path, we would do well as a society to place more importance on the transition from childhood to adulthood among both sexes. Demarcating this time with a ritual might work wonders for many a young person's self-esteem, helping them believe they are being passed life's baton. As a result, they would gain greater control over their time bubble, while fostering greater communal stability.

As it turns out, I am not alone in this thinking. In addition to Laurie's Roots to Branches, a host of companies now offer vision quests for precisely the reasons stated above. Informed by Native American traditions, these outfits typically arrange outings in nature for days to develop mindfulness and resilience among young people. Meanwhile, across the globe, the Dutch practice a related tradition called "dropping" in which they place preteens in a remote part of the forest. Also forced to rely on their wits— as well as teamwork—these children are tasked with finding their way home in the dark.

Though this practice may seem bizarre or even insane, especially to parents who have qualms about letting their kids ride the school bus, the Dutch view it differently. "Children are taught not to depend too much on adults; adults are taught to allow children to solve their own problems," explains Ellen Barry for the *New York Times*. "Droppings distill these principles into extreme form, banking on the idea that even for children who are tired, hungry, and disoriented, there is a compensatory thrill to being in charge."

Bringing Rituals to Business

The need to strengthen communities through rituals also extends to today's companies. For years, business experts have emphasized the importance of strong organizational culture. The late management consultant Peter Drucker, who established the philosophical foundations of the modern corporation once said, "Culture eats strategy for breakfast." He wasn't discounting the need for insightful direction, but was rather insisting on the importance of a powerful set of shared values for collective success. Likewise, Jim Collins, author of *Good to Great: Why Some Companies Make the Leap and Others Don't*, saw a path to excellence beginning and ending with getting the right people in place, cemented by the right culture. "[Great companies] start by getting the right people on the bus, the wrong people off the bus, and the right people in the right seats."

Informed by our continuing discussion on the need for rituals that not only offer group stability, but also contribute to a sense of identity, modern businesses would be well advised to (re)institute rituals into their culture. I make this suggestion based on the ways I have personally observed the efficacies of ritual in my business life. For instance, back when I worked as an emergency physician at St. Francis Hospital in Santa Barbara, California, we had our own rituals. Every morning at 8:00 a.m. one of the sisters would get on the intercom and say something motivating or thoughtful. Also, anytime a baby was born, a chime would play throughout the hospital on the intercom, eliciting smiles.

Though these may be seen as minor observances, they had a big effect on my thinking about leadership. As we have seen, repeated behaviors in the form of rituals offer group cohesion, assuring people of an organization's continuing stability. I took these insights with me when I transitioned into physician management, initially as CEO of First Medical Group, then later as CEO of EmCare

West's one-billion-dollar division of Envision Healthcare. Part of my duties in these roles was conducting meetings in which opinionated physicians wouldn't hold back in giving their thoughts on how to better run the emergency department.

Knowing I had to establish some sort of civility to these discussions or risk losing group buy-in, I reflected upon my experiences with other teams in which I had served, namely soccer clubs. This gave me an idea. How do organized sport clubs keep the peace? They create rituals to reward or punish behavior.

The next week I brought red and yellow cards to my meetings. Whenever someone got out of line or tried to overpower the conversation, I'd give them a yellow card. If they persisted, I'd hand them a red one. This meant that they couldn't say anything any further—they were "out of the game." Now, you might think a roomful of doctors might bristle at something so juvenile. Not at all. My little ritual soon became part of our culture, restoring stability to the team.

In my tenure as a medical executive, I also observed how rituals can lead people away from the Chronos version of time toward Kairos time. One of our physicians who was interested in alternative medicine noticed that before we started meetings our minds were often racing, still working on the last issue we dealt with before convening.

To reinstate focus to our gatherings, he introduced the idea of ringing a chime at the beginning of each meeting. Doing so worked wonderfully. As Eastern practitioners know, the sound of the chime produces a calming effect on the brain. (No wonder it worked so well in the delivery ward.) As soon as we heard it, everybody would quiet down and peacefully listen to it for a few moments. This ritual had a relaxing, reorienting effect on the room, removing distracting thoughts so that we could focus on the meeting.

Rituals to Myths: How Both Work in Concert

Now that we have explored how rituals allow us to transcend our usual conception of time, demarcate life's key phases, and foster solidarity among cultures, including businesses, let's examine how myths strengthen their hold on the collective.

In "Myths and Rituals: A General Theory," an academic paper by Clyde Kluckhohn in the *Harvard Theological Review*, he seeks to learn if myths lead to ritual or the other way around. Reflecting on both throughout history, he comes to see neither as primary:

> Instead, myths and rituals are viewed as related responses to a culturally indicated anxiety over events beyond rational control. The ritual is a repetitive activity in response to a particular threat, while the myth is the rationalization of this activity. The two together thus furnish security systems for the ego, provide means of sublimating in-group aggression, restore individuals to in-group solidarity, and furnish a method of social action against recognized threats.

Following Kluckhohn's logic, there is good reason to at least view ritual as a safeguard against disorder and uncertainty. Columnist Naomi Schalit goes so far as to call it an "anxiety buffer" in a 2017 article for TheConversation.com. "Everyday life is stressful and full of uncertainty. Having a special time of the year when we know exactly what to do, the way we've always done it, provides a comfortable sense of structure, control, and stability."

The holidays offer a good example of Schalit's point. Though recent statistics show the United States is becoming less religious; culturally, we are still connected to the ritual of winter holidays (Christmas, Chanukah, and Kwanzaa). Of course, Christmas looms larger than the others, buttressed by a cadre of myths, including the nativity story and Santa Claus. No matter how it might be commercially exploited for gain, in this instance, both ritual and myth combine to offer the public an unusually strong sense of well-being and unity during this season. Or as Andy Williams sings, *it's the most wonderful time of the year.*

The Power of Stories and Deeds

Returning to the topic of Christmas, let's talk about Santa. Though any kid who grew up believing tales of St. Nick sliding down chimneys with presents in tow is bound to be bummed to learn the truth someday, we shouldn't discount the importance of this myth on our culture. Factual or not, myths possess an indelible purpose, helping to shape our identity. Or as Michael Wood, creator of the PBS series *Myths and Heroes* states, "Myths are as relevant to us today as they were to the ancients. Myths answer timeless questions and serve as a compass to each generation. A myth taps into a universal cultural narrative, the collective wisdom of man."

Seen in this light, starry-eyed children needn't despair upon learning the truth about Santa Claus as they grow up. Instead, they can rejoice in the sense of wonder and magic it once brought them. They can marvel at how it bonded them to their parents and siblings eager to partake in family rituals, like writing a note to the jolly bearded benefactor or leaving out cookies on Christmas Eve. Likewise, parents get to have it both ways. By teaching the myth to their littles ones, they get to relive their youth—while insisting their children behave, lest Santa banish them to the naughty list.

However, for our purposes, there is another element at play here concerning myth and rituals during the holidays. No matter your beliefs, it's not hard to see how these two things offer the stability humans crave in an uncertain world. To understand why, let's return to the aforementioned Friedrich Nietzsche who pronounced,

"God is Dead" in the nineteenth century. He was but one of many thinkers who cast doubt on Christianity, a religion that had long sustained Western culture for millennia.

It may be hard for modern individuals to appreciate the magnitude of this development upon society and the shock waves it produced. Living through this period, the Russian novelist Fyodor Dostoyevsky wrote bestselling novels like *Crime and Punishment* and *The Brothers Karamazov* in which he tried to bring people back to God and the church. Still, in his heart, he despaired this would not be enough to prevent societal collapse. "If it were not for Christ's Church, indeed there would be no restraint on the criminal in his evildoing," he wrote. "If anything protects society even in our time, and even reforms the criminal himself and transforms him into a different person, again it is Christ's law alone, which manifests itself in the acknowledgement of one's own conscience."

Of course, society didn't crumble in the ensuing years. Instead, modern life took shape with science replacing faith as its guide. Though the former offered benefits the latter could not, including technological feats, medical advancements, unprecedented access to information, and the reduction of superstitions that had long held humanity back, a problem remained. Science can offer people the *how*; it can explain reality, giving order to our days. However, it cannot offer us the *why*. It cannot tell us how to live or why we should even go on.

Joseph Campbell recognized this same problem. But to him, myths offered a solution. "Life has no meaning," he once said. "Each of us has meaning and we bring it to life." To better understand Campbell's thinking, we must turn to journalist and commentator Bill Moyers. Moyers interviewed Campbell to create a PBS series entitled *The Power of Myth* in 1987. It proved to be one of the most popular TV series in the history of public television.

In six episodes, they explored cultural and religious mythologies throughout the ages to determine their continuing role in peoples' lives, both then and now.

At one point in their collaboration, Moyers acknowledged how myths can guide us when we are young and impressionable but leave us feeling lost as we age and "begin to know better." Though he was speaking personally, his comments can be seen to reflect how the Age of Enlightenment plunged Western culture into a crisis of meaning with religion's decline. "I understand the yearning," Moyers says:

> In my youth I had fixed stars. They comforted me with their permanence. They gave me a known horizon and they told me there was a loving, kind, and just father out there looking down on me, ready to receive me, thinking of my concerns all the time. Now, Saul Bellow says that science has made a housecleaning of beliefs. But there was value in these things for me. I am today what I am because of those beliefs. I wonder what happens to children who don't have those fixed stars, that known horizon.

What to Do about Our Crisis of Meaning

As a physician and a student of history continually learning and reflecting upon our changing world, I can understand Moyers's concerns. Though he made these comments more than thirty years ago, they are still apt today when so many organizations, structures, and modes of thinking seem to be crumbling before our eyes. Much like Dostoyevsky, we are living in uncertain times threatening stability. Therefore, more than ever, we must rely on our own time bubble to restore balance to our lives. Michael Meade, the author and mythologist, said in an interview with *Pacifica Post*, "Given the dramatic changes going on in the world—and the rapidity of that change—along with 'the rattling and even hollowing out of institutions,' there's not much in the outside world a person can depend upon for orientation and coherence."

Though Meade was not yet aware of the time bubble notion put forward in this book when making his comments, his prescriptive offers shades of it. "We must look inside to find the orientation of our lives and ways to cohere," he says in the same interview. Meade is on to something. There is little we can personally do to control the outside world and all of its uncertainty.

As seen on page 17, all that we as individuals can hope to do in times of upheaval is create a routine offering an individual structure, meaning, and purpose. As a collective, though, it is in our best interest to (re)establish rituals and myths that ground us and offer us solace. Whether it be a civic organization, a religious institution, or a company, its members are best served when establishing hallowed repetitive activities and powerful myths contributing to collective stability. To understand how some of the longest persisting organizations in history managed to accomplish such a feat throughout the ages, we now turn our attention to the topic of tradition.

CHAPTER 6

Tradition!

FREEMASONRY HAS RECEIVED A LOT OF ATTENTION in the last few years. All manner of conspiracy stories have circulated the web about the Masons. Meanwhile, incendiary movies like *National Treasure* and books like *The DaVinci Code* by Dan Brown have only fueled the fire. Yet even before Internet memes and YouTube videos flooded the public consciousness, popular entertainment traded jokes about this mysterious group.

In *The Simpsons* episode "Homer the Great," which first aired in January 1995, Homer joins an ancient secret society called the Stonecutters. His new fraternity sings a ditty summarizing popular suspicions with these funny, yet provocative lyrics: *Who controls the British crown?/Who keeps the metric system down?/We do, we do/Who keeps Atlantis off the maps?/Who keeps the Martians under wraps?/*

We do, we do/Who holds back the electric car?/Who makes Steve Guttenberg a star? We do, we do.

As with so many things, the truth about Masonry is more complicated. No one knows the group's true origins. "Due to the secretive nature of this society, coupled with the fact that relatively few pieces of literature have survived over time which could have told us more about how Freemasonry came into being, it's difficult to point an exact moment in time and space when this unique organization came into existence," explains MasonicFind.com.

Nevertheless, Masonry happens to be the largest and oldest fraternity in existence, numbering in the millions worldwide. In continuing our discussion on how rituals and myths contribute to the stability we humans crave, we will investigate how this group, and another—Judaism—the oldest of the monotheist faiths, have managed to persist throughout the millennia despite untold threats.

So, what's the key to these groups' longevity in spite of dramatic changes across time, continents, and among peoples? As we shall see, both share something in common: an insistence on the importance of tradition. But first, the Masons.

Traversing the Shadowy Mists of Time

Though modern Freemasonry began with the founding of the Grand Lodge in London, England, in 1717, the story goes further back. "A widely accepted theory among Masonic scholars is that [the organization] arose from Stonemason guilds during the Middle Ages," according to the Geneva Masonic Lodge.

Jack Hennings, past Worshipful Master of Laguna Lodge 672 concurs. According to him, the original Freemasons consisted of builder guilds possessing uncommon knowledge. "In the days of the construction of Solomon's Temple, we find Hiram Abiff, sometimes regarded as the first Freemason," says Hennings. "He and his brothers had skills 99 percent of the population lacked. Not only did they know how to construct stately edifices, they could read and write, skills only kings and nobles had back then."

Masonry's Life Blood

Although Freemasonry professes no particular religion, it contains traditions bearing similarities to an organized faith. Freemasons meet in a temple called a lodge, in homage to where their forebears once gathered. "Immense symbolism permeates any lodge," says Hennings.

> The furnishings are arranged to facilitate our rituals. At mine, we also have a dining room for developing brotherly love. We meet here every Thursday at 6:00 p.m. to eat a meal together prepared by the brothers. Our stewards purchase the food, cook it, and serve the group. Every week I follow the same routine because I appreciate the opportunity to be around like-minded people, I call brothers. I am as close to these men as I am my own brothers. In fact, my wife says I can't be buried on Thursday because I'd be at lodge.

Masonic code also provides routine structures to proceedings. No less than seven Master Masons must be present to transact the business of a meeting, which can include raising candidates to degrees in this order: Entered Apprentice, Fellowcraft, and Master Mason. There are also other appendant bodies to Freemasonry, with their own degrees. (Sidenote: The phrase "giving someone the third degree," which once pertained to the intense grilling one might receive in a police interrogation, is believed to originate from the interrogation ceremonies involved in the final Masonic degree.)

More traditions abound concerning the brothers' attire. Once upon a time, the Stonemasons of yore, also known as Operant Masons, toiled in constructing the structures described earlier. In time, the group began accepting men from other professions to encourage intellectual diversity. These became known as "Free and Accepted" Masons. They later came to outnumber the Operant Masons due to changing economic circumstances.

These days, so-called Speculative Freemasons wear aprons in honor of their Stonemason brethren called Operative Masons. To understand why, we may consult FreeMasons.org: "An apron was worn by Operative Masons to protect themselves from rough stones and tools. Presently, it is a badge of fraternal distinction. During his first degree, each Mason is given a plain white leather apron. It represents the white lambskin, a symbol of innocence."

Go to any lodge the world over and you will notice that Masons love decorating these aprons. Their sacred pinafores often feature bedazzling accoutrements, including intricate needlepoint depictions of ancient heroic deeds, literary allusions, religious connotations, nationalistic flags, family crests, and a host of iconic symbology, like the compass and square. Beyond being requisite apparel for meetings, aprons figure prominently upon a brother's death. "It is the initial gift of Freemasonry to a candidate, and at the end of life's pilgrimage it is reverently placed on his mortal remains and buried with his body in the grave," according to MasonicWorld.com.

Behavioral Traditions

Just as important as what Masons wear is the conduct they live by. As we have seen throughout this book, consistency is key to attain and maintain individual and group stability. On every continent but Antarctica, you will find the same officer hierarchy no matter if the brothers speak Greek or Russian. Stephanie Watson describes this hierarchy for HowStuffWorks.com:

> Officers of the Lodge include a Master (referred to as "Worshipful Master"), a Senior Warden (who helps the Master with his duties and takes over when the Master is away), a Junior Warden (who ensures that visiting Masons have the correct credentials), a Treasurer (who collects dues and pays the Lodge's bills), a Secretary (who records meeting minutes and handles other administrative duties), a Senior Deacon (who guides visitors and new members into the Lodge), and a Junior Deacon (who serves as messenger of the lodge).

The Stories We Tell Unite Us

Harkening back to the importance of mythmaking discussed on pages 73–76, a consistent ideology bridges lodges separated by oceans and languages. Three ideas compose the central tenets of Freemasonry: brotherly love, relief, and truth.

If these ideas sound familiar, that's no accident. They are important themes informing the codification of our republic. In fact, Americans owe a great deal to Masonry for the founding of our democracy. Writing for *JSTOR Daily*, Peter Feuerherd explains why:

> George Washington reached the top level of the Masons on August 4, 1753, securing the leadership of the influential lodge in Alexandria, Virginia. Washington was not alone among the founding founders; some scholars say as many as twenty-one signers of the Declaration of Independence were Masons. Many historians note that the Constitution

and the Bill of Rights both seem to be heavily influenced by the Masonic 'civic religion,' which focuses on freedom, free enterprise, and a limited role for the state.

In this same article, Feuerherd makes the point that nowadays Masonic meetings are seen by the public as innocuous gatherings of men wishing to congregate for the social purposes Hennings describes. However, Masonry's impact in cultivating democracy is often overlooked.

In Europe, the Masons were known for plotting against royal governments. In America, they became known for promoting Republican virtues of self-government. Masonic thought influenced American history: The Masons were opposed to the claims of royalty—a strong influence on the development of the American revolt against Britain which culminated in the Revolutionary War. They were also known for their opposition to the Catholic Church, another international organization that competed for allegiance.

Due to Masonic influence on the establishment of our country, including its myths and ideals, it is little wonder so many brothers have occupied high-ranking positions in government. Since the establishment of the presidential office in 1789, we have had forty-six presidents. It's staggering to realize that of this number, fourteen are known Freemasons, including James Monroe, Andrew Jackson, Franklin D. Roosevelt, Harry S. Truman, Lyndon Johnson, and Gerald Ford. Senate majority leader Chuck Schumer is a Freemason. So is Bob Dole. There have also been numerous Mason supreme court justices, including Earl Warren, Potter C. Stewart, and Thurgood Marshall.

Mason Enemies: Within and Without

Despite Masonry's many accomplishments and well-placed members, the organization has long been the target of persecution. At the beginning of the American republic, opposition reached its peak with the establishment of a political party against the group. "Opponents of this society seized upon the uproar to create the Anti-Masonic Party," according to *Encyclopedia Britannica*. "It was the first American third party, the first political party to hold a national nominating convention, and the first to offer the electorate a platform of party principles."

John Quincy Adams, our nation's sixth president, was particularly determined to stamp out Masonry due to what has been known as "The Morgan Affair." What happened was William Morgan, a onetime Mason, became an outspoken critic of the group. Long before the Internet would divulge most, if not all, of Freemasonry's secrets, Morgan was intent on publishing a book to expose his brothers. When Morgan suddenly went missing, many prominent groups condemned Masons for killing Morgan as retribution. The scandal reached a fever pitch as numerous individuals and organizations denounced the organization for perceived elitism.

Ultimately, the Anti-Masons offered an important third-party alternative to (Mason) Andrew Jackson's Democrats, but their influence soon waned as the brouhaha ebbed. Still, the event had a powerful impact on Masonry. "Scandals like the Morgan affair, along with the decrees issued by the Catholic Church, going back to the 1700s, helped to reduce Masonry's public standing," according to Hennings. In the wake of these incidents, as well as criticisms from without and within, the group adopted more of a focus on religious-inspired rituals. "I would say Freemasonry at this point became more Christian-centered," says Hennings. "It went from being a kind of partying club with lots of drinking to something more dignified with its ideal of male self-improvement. In fact, our motto is 'We make good men better.'"

A Tradition of Persecution

Before the political threats and the Morgan affair, Masonry had detractors. The strongest institution in Western Europe viewed Masonry as a threat. "To understand why the Catholic Church resented us, it's helpful to tell the story of the Knights Templar," says Hennings. "Many people had never heard of this mysterious group until the movie *Indiana Jones and the Last Crusade*, but its roots go back to the Middle Ages and its story is intertwined with Masonry."

After Christian soldiers took control of Jerusalem during the First Crusade, groups of pilgrims sought to visit the Holy Land. But they ran into a problem. "Many were killed while crossing through Muslim-controlled territory during their journey," explains Jennie Cohen, writing for History.com. "Around 1118, a French knight named Hugues de Payens founded a military order along with eight relatives and acquaintances, calling it the Poor Knights of the Temple of King Solomon (later known as the Knights Templar). With the support of Baldwin II, the king of Jerusalem, they set up headquarters on the sacred Temple Mount and pledged to protect Christian visitors to the city."

Like the Masons (some of which were rumored to compose the Templar ranks), this newly empowered group benefitted from advantages that the largely ignorant and illiterate masses did not possess. For one thing, they were organized. They also had fighting skills and uncommon knowledge, leading to demand for their services. They soon became mercenaries paid to escort vulnerable people to the Holy Land.

Around this time, the Templars adopted their own traditions, including an austere code of conduct that came to be known as chivalry. They also developed their own style of dress: white habits emblazoned with a red cross. Sensing the benefits that might accrue from utilizing these knights for their bidding, the Catholic Church came to embrace the group for a time. It didn't hurt that Bernard of Clairvaux, a prominent abbot, formally endorsed the band of fighters.

Soon, the order began raking in new recruits and lavish donations, leading to its growing influence. "Now numbering in the thousands, the Templars established new chapters throughout Western Europe," again writes Cohen. "They also set up a network of banks that enabled religious pilgrims to deposit assets in their home countries and withdraw funds in the Holy Land. Along with their donated fortune and various business ventures, this system gave the Knights Templar enormous financial sway." It seemed like everything was going the Templars' way. Until King Philip IV got involved.

A Day That Will Live in Infamy

For years, Philip IV had a problem with the Templars. He resented going to them to finance his battles. He hated that he owed them more money than he had. Determined to wipe them out and steal their wealth, he targeted Jacques De Molay, their grand master. Under pretenses of offering De Molay another crusade, the king tricked him into lowering his defenses. Then Philip IV ordered De Molay and his leadership arrested. For seven years, Philip's minions tortured De Molay for false confessions to bring down his group.

At last, the day arrived when Philip, in concert with Pope Clement, intended to publicly execute De Molay. Philip's men read the charges against De Molay and his brothers in front of Paris's

Notre Dame Cathedral. These offenses included heresy, homosexuality, and corruption. The sentence? Death by burning at the stake. Instead of capitulating, De Molay proclaimed his innocence and the innocence of his organization. Enraged at such insolence, Philip ordered De Molay set on fire. As the flames lapped at his body, De Molay issued a curse upon his tormentors: "Let evil swiftly befall those who have wrongly condemned us. God will avenge our death."

There is a reason why Friday the 13th is considered unlucky. This event occurred on Friday, October 13, 1307. And, as it turns out, De Molay's dying curse proved true. "Pope Clement V, complicit by design or cowardice, was dead thirty-three days later—from a severe bout of dysentery brought about by advanced bowel cancer," writes Jamie Seidel for the *Daily Telegraph*. "King Philip IV of France, who had been happy to kill and defame Christendom's defenders for their wealth and land, died within eight months. This time it was a hunting accident."

Whether or not De Molay's enemies met their end due to De Molay's invocation is not our place to say. What matters is that in the ensuing years, Templars would swell the ranks of the Masons as they were driven underground. "It was very easy for the Freemason leadership of the time to give the Templars cover and help them to blend into their community because they shared values and practiced similar traditions," says Hennings.

These days, Freemasonry even has an auxiliary Templar degree within the York Rite. "I have that degree," says Hennings. "They call me Sir Jack. Yes, I'm a Knights Templar as well as a Freemason."

* * *

"Without tradition, our lives would be as shaky as a fiddler on the roof," says Tevye, the protagonist in the musical *Fiddler on the Roof.*

Based on short stories written in Yiddish by Sholem Aleichem, with music by Jerry Bock and lyrics by Sheldon Harnick, *Fiddler* struck a chord with mainstream audiences (no pun intended). This humorous yet sad tale was the first of its kind to depict the hardships of Eastern European Jewish shtetl life.

Unfortunately, this is but one story in a long tale of persecution against the Jews throughout history. As discussed on page 62, my mother endured her share of misfortune in the Holocaust in which six million Jews perished. Though this horrific event looms large in the public mind, bolstered by Academy Award fare such as *Schindler's List* and most recently *Jo Jo Rabbit*, it is but one of many acts of genocide and cruelty that have plagued the Jewish people. "Yet, despite so many persistent threats over the years, the Jews have managed to survive largely as a result of their unwavering commitment to tradition as a source of comfort and identity," explains Rabbi Jeffrey Stiffman, the long-serving religious leader of Shaare Emeth Temple in St. Louis, Missouri.

A Long History of Oppression

Judaism dates back nearly four thousand years. Adherents believe in one God, a loving deity who communicates through prophets and rewards good deeds while punishing evil. According to the Torah, the Jews' holy book, the first such prophet was Abraham. God revealed himself to him who later established the religion. Abraham and his descendants believe their Lord made a special covenant or promise with them that their descendants were chosen people who would generate a great nation.

Like any major religion, it is hard to put into words the complexities of its people, culture, and heritage. The Religious Literacy Project at Harvard Divinity School explains:

Judaism embraces the intricate religious and cultural development of the Jewish people through more than thirty centuries of history, stretching from Biblical times to medieval Spain to the Enlightenment, and then to the Holocaust and the founding of the modern state of Israel. From a religious perspective Judaism is a theistic system, but from a peoplehood perspective, it is also the group memory of the manifold communities and cultures formed by Jews through the ages.

Still, it is clear that Judaism has historically come under attack from local power structures. For context, Beth Daley, writing for TheConversation.com, weighs in on this long-standing phenomenon. "Antisemitism has been called history's oldest hatred and it has shown itself to be remarkably adaptable. It is carved from—and sustained by—powerful precedents and inherited stereotypes."

Daley references early instances of oppression as far back as the Roman stateman Cicero denouncing Jews in the first century BC for meddling in civil affairs. She also points out another contemporary's aversion to their traditions. "The Roman historian Tacitus, c. 56–120 AD, was contemptuous of 'base and abominable' Jewish customs and was deeply disturbed by those of his compatriots who had renounced their ancestral gods and converted to Judaism."

In *Judeophobia: Attitudes Toward the Jews in the Ancient World*, German scholar of ancient religions Peter Schafer also seeks context to explain the harmful stereotypes and hatred Daley describes. In his 1988 book, he points to the exclusive nature of the Jewish faith, its insistence on being labeled a "chosen people," and its refusal to abandon its long-held traditions of the sabbath, dietary prescriptions, and the practice of circumcision as the male observance of God's covenant.

Like the Masons, the Jews also came under fire in the Middle Ages under institutionalized discrimination by the church. Scapegoating formed a major part of the problem with the widespread belief that Jews were to blame for the murder of Jesus, their savior. Throughout much of this period, Jews were often forbidden from marrying Christians, appearing as witnesses against Christians in courts, and holding government positions. Further feeding the flames of hatred were outlandish stories put forth by one Thomas of Monmouth, a monk who lived at Norwich Cathedral Priory in the mid-twelfth century. In a series of writings, he put forth the tale that Jews possessed horns and tails, and blamed them for the mysterious death of a Christian child.

Tradition as Remedy for Displacement

Though an entire book could be devoted to cataloging atrocities perpetuated against the Jews, for our purposes, we will zero in on just one example that comes from Rabbi Stiffman. Though every American schoolchild knows 1492 to be the year Christopher Columbus set sail across the Atlantic, ending up in North America, something else of import occurred in Columbus's home country at this time.

While Columbus was busy searching for spices, King Ferdinand and Queen Isabella decided to expel the Jews from Spain. "Up until then, Jews had had a long-standing, very creative, and affluent community," Rabbi Stiffman explains. "It included many philosophers, poets, and scientists. Yet, when the Catholics defeated the Muslims, the royal family decided all the non-Christians should be removed. The crown decreed all Jews either convert, flee, or be killed."

A period of great migration, called the Diaspora, resulted from these orders. Many Jews settled in North Africa, among Muslim countries, and in parts of the Middle East. Some went north, too. In the 1700s, Holland became an open country where people were judged by what they did rather than their religion. The so-called Sephardic Jews, who descended from these exiles, settled in other countries and did fairly well.

Others who couldn't leave Spain for their own reasons became known as "Hidden Jews." The Spanish term for these individuals became Marrano, meaning "pig." This derogatory label led to further prejudice. To avoid retaliation, many remaining Jews ostensibly became Catholics while secretly practicing Judaism. "A number of these survived by practicing their traditions in private and making no public display of their religion," explains Rabbi Stiffman. These traditions included surreptitiously keeping a kosher diet, celebrating the sabbath or "shabbat" as it is called, and observing special occasions, including the high holidays: Yom Kippur and Rosh Hashanah.

When word of this clandestine Jewish insurrection reached the authorities, they were furious. Redoubling their efforts to crush such insolence, they embarked upon an inquisition. Coordinated by religious authorities and aimed at rooting out secret practitioners, agents took serious measures. "They would send spies to see whether a woman washed all of her table linens on a Friday so she could set a fancy table for Shabbat," says Rabbi Stiffman. "They would also check to see if candles were lit in the homes on the same day." Such draconian actions forced many so-called Marranos to observe their services and celebrations in basements. "These 'Crypto-Jews' helped keep the Jewish traditions going— and thus, Judaism itself going—through the centuries."

Tradition as Antidote for Chaos
Before we close this chapter, let us recall how we have witnessed the practice of routine contributing to the stability of individuals and

groups, offering them identity, purpose, and meaning. We labeled the term "time bubble" to explain the content we use to structure our days. Now, it's time to reflect on how aspects of the time bubble can be used to stave off the worst exigencies life may present. "The Jewish essayist Ahad Ha'am once said, 'Even as Israel has kept the Sabbath, so the Sabbath has kept Israel,'" says Rabbi Stiffman. "Observing the Sabbath—whether it involved the family coming together for dinner, joining for prayer, or going to the synagogue for prayer—actually helped keep the Jewish people alive."

To understand Rabbi Stiffman's logic, it is helpful to recognize that the act of observing traditions was something that separated the Jewish people from their neighbors. For a long time, persecuted Jews lived in closed-off communities called ghettos where they had very little to call their own. What money they managed to earn they would save all week to have a Friday night dinner and maybe a Saturday lunch. "This practice made the Shabbat Sabbath a very special, very sacred time," explains Rabbi Stiffman.

During these moments, isolated Jews—*persecuted Jews*—spent their time studying the Torah, praying together, socializing, and developing a community they could count on, especially in times of difficulty. "As a result, home traditions became important. The lighting of the candles, the blessing of the wine and bread (challah)—all of this became a force for uniting families. Together, these people shared a human experience both hopeful and joyful, unlike much of their daily drudgery."

These days, only a small percentage of Jews observe many of the traditions Rabbi Stiffman describes. Yet, once upon a time, the majority of Jews observed all dietary laws. Likewise, they kept up Shabbat every week and even refrained from working on Saturdays. Though the world has changed, the need for tradition has not. As group experiences demonstrate for both the Masons and the Jews, traditions can serve as an antidote to chaos.

Like the myths and rituals observed in Chapter 5 (page 65), traditions offer us a sense of regularity. They serve as protection against the gnawing uncertainty plaguing so many of us throughout our days, especially when facing something as frightening, traumatic, and unprecedented as a pandemic. Traditions also give us a sense of stability, leading to balance and order. Or as Rabbi Stiffman explains, "Yes, the practice of tradition provides a comforting feeling of nostalgia. On the other hand, it grounds us as people, no matter what group we happen to belong to. No matter what crisis we face, including COVID-19."

Last but not least, the practice of routine gives us a sense of identity in a world where many of us constantly seek to understand our place and path. "As a human, I want to know who I am," says Rabbi Stiffman. "I also want to know *what* I am. I want to return to certain regular customs, ceremonies, and ideas in my life that make me feel comfortable because they are a part of me."

Now that we have seen how traditions can provide us with balance, order, and structure, as well as help to shape our sense of self, let's turn our attention to the subject of the next chapter: how routines can make us better than we ever thought possible. It's now time to learn how the right time bubble can transform us into higher performing individuals.

CHAPTER 7

Only Keith Can
Bust the Crust

IT'S A THURSDAY AFTERNOON IN MAY and Chucky Klapow is making last-minute preparations for the Rolling Stones to play at Dublin's Croke Park. One of Europe's largest stadiums, it often plays host to Ireland's biggest events. Within hours it will house no less than 82,300 screaming fans eager to witness a group of long-haired entertainers once described as "uglier, scruffier versions of the Beatles."

Point of context: the Stones received this comment in 1964. They have since gone on to thrive for five more decades. And while the Beatles broke up and other contemporaries died or faded into irrelevance, the Stones are going strong. Not only have they been accepted by the mainstream (witness front man Mick Jagger's 2003 knighting), they still command army-sized audiences even though their youngest member, Ronnie Wood, is in his early seventies.

Based on the history of the Stones, the vast number of expected attendees—and, of course, all the money riding on tonight—Chucky should be a tad freaked. After all, he's the band's choreographer, charged with ensuring the final leg of *The Rolling Stones European No Filter Tour*, their first appearance in Ireland in more than a decade, goes off without a hitch. To be fair, Chucky has good reason to fret. Though the thirty-eight-year-old came to prominence managing the Disney channel's High School Musical franchise, handling a Stones gig is like nothing else on Earth.

Reining in the Insanity

Unlike most rock spectacles, Stones shows still feel fraught with danger. Though Altamont occurred years ago, Stones performances have never been of the cuddly variety. Guitarist Keith Richards used to carry a gun to shows to protect himself from rioting fans. Regardless, the tension at any performance cannot help but be exacerbated by the band members' ages; they are all septuagenarians with drummer Charlie Watts, the oldest, pushing eighty. Not only is it shocking that the four principal players can remain on the road while many in their age group reside in nursing homes, but they also still manage to consistently perform at stratospheric levels. How is this possible?

"It all comes down to routine," says Klapow. "Without it, we'd be lost." As the following shall demonstrate, a well-constructed time bubble is key to consistent excellent performance, whether you are an aging rock star, the CEO of a major publicly traded company, a professional race car driver—or whether you're like the rest of us mere mortals, grinding it out daily. No matter who you are, the secret achievement sauce is comprised of structure, preparation, and discipline.

Time Bubble Excellence

The Stones continue to function as the world's greatest rock performers due to their musical passion and a time bubble of detail-driven precision that rivals a Pentagon-level military invasion. Sharing their story of personal development ties into the other promise of this book: how to maximize your life through routine. And while the appeal of any Stones show lies in its visceral punch: its heart-pumping jams, its intimations of sexual promiscuity, its ability to hurl you out of your seat to dance along with a chicken-strutting Mick Jagger—the band's performances are never left to chance.

Tonight, as with every performance, the guys are set to converge onstage at precisely 8:50 p.m. with Keith hitting his first guitar riff at 9:00 p.m. sharp. Prior to the actual live event, preparations began more than a year ago. The stage and construction crews have been building platforms and catwalks for a week. For the last few days, a gaffing cadre has been repositioning Kliegs, simultaneously sound-rigging every square inch of the venue for optimal acoustics.

Meanwhile, behind the scenes of stage construction, the Stones have been quietly preparing for success in Dublin. As hammers flew and beams went up at the Croke, the foursome conducted the same routine they use when approaching any new city. Though their private plane touched down a day ago, little time was spent relaxing. Instead, Mick went to work. "One of the most significant things Mick does regularly, no matter where we are, is conduct a one-hour meeting with a local language and culture expert," says Klapow.

Leaving Nothing to Chance

Though Mick's in-concert remarks come off as effortless and clever, the truth is he takes great pains to become an insider. The night before the show, he sat with a local Dublin expert to get a lay of the land. "It's important for him to be able to communicate with the audience and speak their language, to talk about things happening around town," says Chucky. "Mick is a true entertainer. Therefore, it's not just about doing the songs and singing them well. It's about connecting with the audience on *every* level." To this end, Mick spent last night planning what he'll say in concert, including when in the set-list he will say it. "You should hear him in China," says Chucky.

At last, 4 p.m. finally hits: *showtime.* With hours to go before the concert starts, the guys are following their routine. On the hour, the band's motorcade (a forty-five-person entourage) leaves the hotel for the venue. As the caravan of vehicles carrying each member of the band, their personal security, assistants, and family members (including grandchildren) winds itself to a stop outside the heavily secured loading garage, any vestiges of Croke Park, Dublin, or even Ireland for that matter, dissolve.

Like a soap bubble that exists but a moment, the backstage to this stadium and everything within transforms for a brief speck of time. Constructed with absolute punctiliousness, the Stones' surroundings, known to band and crew as "the compound," become the familiar; an exact replica of every venue they have ever played. Composed of dressing rooms, hair and makeup rooms, a reception area, and containing a vocal/dance rehearsal studio, this mobile structure suddenly assumes the exact layout, look, and feel of every floor plan in every city along the tour.

Welcome to the Stones' Traveling Time Bubble

Upon arrival, familiar faces of the backstage crew greet the band members and entourage, guiding them in. "Each of their rooms is the same in every city we go to down to the furniture," says Klapow.

"It's the same couch, the same carpeting, the same drapery whether we're playing at Arrowhead in Kansas City or AT&T in Dallas." But the bubble goes further, deeper. The very scent of the rooms is the same. "It's identical in every single city. Even the music. They have speakers in their dressing rooms. Usually there's jazz playing in Charlie's room and Keith jams Chuck Berry or Little Richard."

At 4:30 p.m., the band assembles for sound check. "Like the backstage compound, the stage has to be the same environment so that when they step up there, they're home," says Klapow. Tape marks guide them to the location of towels and water bottles. Everything has to be in exactly the same place all the time. As usual, Mick walks the stage today, hunting for imperfections. "There," he says, pointing to a dangerous corner where a plug sticks out too far. "Don't want to trip on that."

According to Chucky, the band and crew use this time to double check that everything is the way it's supposed to be. "A lot of people would say, 'Okay, I don't need to go up there and sound check or anything like that. We've done this a million times. It's going to be fine,'" says Klapow. "But this is part of the routine. It's what goes into making a good show. You do everything the way you're supposed to do it and then everything falls into place."

Almost Showtime

Sound check promptly ends at 5:00 p.m. and Mick heads to wardrobe. A meeting ensues for fifteen minutes in which he and his stylist pick out the outfits he will wear. From 5:30 p.m. to 6:30 p.m. Mick meets with the teleprompter operator to review the script he wrote the night before. Additionally, he confirms that any foreign language portions are spelled out phonetically, so he never makes a mistake.

At 6:30 p.m. Mick receives a thirty-minute hair and makeup session. Afterward, from 7:00 p.m. to 7:10 p.m., the band does a quick meet and greet. The tour coordinator brings the band to a reception area where a line is already waiting. The visitation goes fast. "It's just walk in, say hi, take a picture, and out," says Klapow. "The guys don't do big meet and greets; it's only for major contest winners, the arena or stadium owner, or sponsors of the tour."

From 7:10 p.m. to 7:20 p.m., Mick does a quick change, switching out his stage clothes for more comfortable warm-up clothing. Even though Mick performed vocal warm-ups in the car on the ride over and at sound check, he uses the next fifty minutes to practice vocal exercises alone in his dressing room. "You hear him singing the entire time," Klapow recalls. "It's pretty cool. He's very committed to that routine. He doesn't break from that rhythm. He never takes the attitude, 'I don't need to warm up now.' He does it every time."

Stones fans know that Mick's singing is only half the fun of any concert. True showman that he is, the seventy-six-year-old front man delivers a cardiovascular-packed danceathon of preening, thrusting, hopping, kicking, and generally flying around the stage to the crowd's delight. Routine plays no small part in this stage-craft element either. From 8:10 p.m. to 8:30 p.m., Mick works with his physiotherapist and Chucky to explore what Klapow calls his "dance vocabulary." In every single backstage compound an area is set up as a little dance studio. The floor is smooth with ample space to accommodate Jagger's famous moves. It's also set up with speakers for Chucky to plug in his computer and play the music.

"I'm kinda like the DJ for that session," says Kaplow. "He'll warm up for two or three songs and then for the fourth song we'll turn the volume way up and just jam. I never tell Mick what to do. I just pay attention to all the things he does naturally. He has so many cool moves that he does organically and I'll just keep cycling through all of his options. The last thing I want him to do is go on stage and just get stuck clapping or strutting, pointing and clapping. He has so many other moves in his arsenal and I want to make sure he doesn't forget any of them."

While Mick's busy warming up, Keith enjoys his own routine. It's the same thing in every single city, every single show: Keith has a shepherd's pie delivered to his dressing room. No matter if you're a bandmate or crew, all are welcome to share. However, participation comes with a stipulation. Keith must be the first one to cut into the top layer. Or as Mick says, "Only Keith can bust the crust."

Action!
From 8:30 p.m. to 8:45 p.m., Mick returns to his dressing room for final prep. He changes back into his show clothes, slips on his opening jacket, attaches his mic battery pack, and puts in his in-ear monitors. At 8:45 p.m., the band does a quick photo session with the opening act and then it's truly showtime. "At this point, I go to the stage, put in my earplugs, and situate myself in front. I'm always in the same spot, next to the thrust, stage right. I wear the same yellow sweatshirt every single show, so Mick knows exactly where I am. Not that he needs me. I'm definitely an extra energy source just to remind him but it's fun when you have someone to keep you pumped up."

Despite so much discussion concerning doing things the same way, tonight's performance does offer a rare break in routine. It's something small but meaningful to this band who started out so long ago in the pubs of London. Rather than beginning with Richards's guitar riff from "Start Me Up," the show starts with a single spotlight on Charlie Watts, seated alone onstage, while Richards plays the menacing chords to "Sympathy for the Devil." From his vantage point Klapow notices something you might miss in the sea of people. For a second, Watts breaks character, making bug-eyes to Jagger offstage. His usual controlled mien transforms into the widest of grins as if to say, "Can you believe we're still doing this?"

* * *

Much like the routineology force-field protecting the globe-trotting Stones, NASCAR Hall of Famer and four-time Cup champion Jeff Gordon lived thirty-eight weeks a year for more than two decades in his own hermetically sealed time bubble. Routine-abiding to Jeff was a life-or-death matter. Careening around a racetrack at speeds approaching two hundred miles per hour required strict adherence to the tiniest detail. "If I didn't get it exactly right, I might not be here today," says Gordon.

Parental Influence

Preservation aside, Gordon also attributes his success as a high performer to the routine indoctrination his stepfather and mentor John Bickford gave him as a boy. Like the Stones, Jeff was expected to be in a strange place day after day to compete. "I've always said athletes need to know how to travel," says Bickford.

In order to make sure his stepson didn't get thrown by so much changing stimuli, Bickford instilled in him a kind of internal discipline—a mental game. "At the end of the day there are a lot of people out there talented physically, whether it be Lebron James in basketball or Tom Brady in football. What makes a professional is someone who gets into the cerebral part of the game. Someone who can remain unflustered and focused in spite of all that's coming at them," says Bickford.

Routine Pays Off

Taking Bickford's advice to heart, Gordon advanced to unprecedented levels in the race car world. Beginning with the Busch Series with Hugh Connerty Racing, he snatched three impressive wins, leading to a full-time spot in the Cup Series for Hendrick Motorsports in 1993. A four-time Sprint Cup Champion, he clinched four titles in 1995, 1997, 1998, and 2001. Gordon is ranked third on the all-time Cup wins list with a whopping ninety-three victories. A three-time Daytona winner, he was named one of the "50 Greatest Drivers" by NASCAR and the "Fifth Best Driver of All Time" by Fox Sports.

Still, no matter how well Gordon performed, Bickford's words of routine were never far from his thoughts. They followed Gordon every step of his competitive life. "I had a routine for how I buckled into the car seat, how I put on my helmet," Gordon says. "I'd always do it in a certain order, so I didn't forget anything. First, my lap belt. Then crotch belt. Left shoulder belt. Right shoulder belt. Then the head and neck support, earpieces, nose strip to help me breathe a little better, and eye drops for moisture in my eyes. Helmet. Gloves. Then steering wheel. There's a mark that lines it up to the steering column preset from the day before. I'd give it a good tug to make sure it was on nice and tight."

Rinse and Repeat

Like Klapow and the Stones, Bickford became a master at recreating the same physical location for Jeff in every city. Jeff's motor coach became his version of the Stones' compound with Bickford ensuring the environment offered consistency. The last thing Bickford wanted was for his stepson to encounter surprises that might affect his mental game. "Whether Jeff was competing at Bristol or Michigan or Vegas or Phoenix, everything was set up exactly the same," he says. After the race, Jeff would get on a plane and then the coach manager would drive the coach to the next location. It literally became his home away from home. And as such, it had to remain constant. Every detail was precise, from the positioning of the bowl of fruit, to the television, everything was set up exactly the same. I made sure we had the same food again and again in the refrigerator."

Even though most people outside racing might not recognize Bickford, his role was fundamental in shaping Gordon's wins. While drivers like Gordon occupy much of the spotlight, high performers rely on a team in much the same way the Stones lean on Klapow and others. It's also important to know when it comes to NASCAR, competition occurs between teams—not the actual drivers. Accordingly, each team member has a specific role to play and a team's synchronicity leads to its efficiency, productivity, and ultimately, its success.

"The best teams have a rhythm," says Gordon. "Every coach or person responsible for performance will tell you that the best thing for any athlete is their rhythm, and your routine helps you get into your rhythm." According to Gordon, his rhythm became his routine. "Once I was in my rhythm, I really didn't pay any attention to who I was passing, I was just in a zone. People who are unsuccessful—they just don't have that rhythm."

* * *

Angel Martinez also knows a thing or two about rhythm. Until his retirement in 2017, he served as chairman of the board of Deckers Brands, beginning in 2008 as its CEO. Prior to this, he presided as its president for three years. Designers, marketers, and distributors of footwear, apparel, and accessories, Deckers is well known for big-name brands such as Ugg, Hoka, and Teva. Before joining Deckers, Martinez cofounded Reebok where he held senior positions, including president and CEO of Rockport, one of Reebok's largest subsidiaries.

Inauspicious Beginnings

Though clearly a high-performing success in the world of business, Martinez didn't have anything handed to him. Instead, he rose through the ranks based on intelligence and self-enforced routine. A native from Cuba, he didn't see his parents for more than thirty-four years. His grandmother's sister and her husband adopted him when he was three years old before fleeing to the United States. Unfortunately, the Cuban revolution prevented his immediate family from joining him in the South Bronx for decades. Bereft of a traditional support system and wanting to make his parents proud back home, Martinez vowed to succeed. Like how racing filled a hole in Gordon's life, running was Martinez's salvation. Once he realized he had a talent for it, he honed his skills through routine.

"The summer of my freshman year, I decided I was going to run five miles every single day," says Martinez. To hold himself accountable, he pledged to himself that if he missed his quota, he would run ten miles to make up for it. It wasn't easy sticking to this routine. "I had a job where I remember getting off at 4:30 p.m. From there, I would go home, and by 5:00 p.m., I was off and running. I really had to hustle, too, because I had another job that began at 7:00 p.m., and I didn't want to miss putting in the five miles I promised myself."

Self-Made Man

Such dedication and perseverance paid off. Martinez earned a scholarship to the University of California, Davis, where he studied rhetoric and marketing while still running competitively. "What I discovered about running back then was that I had to do the same thing every day in order to improve. Running is not like going to baseball practice three to five times a week. What you do in that sport might vary in practice daily. Whereas in running, if you want to improve, you have to run the miles. So, in time, it just becomes by its own nature, a routine-driven activity."

Still, Martinez never dreamed that running would take him so far. After graduating college, he used his education, his zeal for the sport, and his routine-minded work ethic to open running-shoe stores in Mountain View and Alameda, California. Soon after, he cofounded Reebok. Though Reebok flourished for a time, Martinez soon realized that the skills he developed for success weren't being used by everyone in his organization.

Since stepping away from his previous role, Martinez can contemplate the company, its achievements, and its failures, with greater perspective. "Routine requires discipline," remarks Martinez. "In the early days of Reebok, I would argue that the organization was extremely undisciplined."

Routine Needed

Martinez, who only escaped unbelievable poverty through his own dedication to routine, quickly saw that such a lack of discipline was destined to sink the ship he had built. Though Reebok managed to stay in business, eventually being absorbed by a subsidiary of Adidas, Martinez knew that he needed a fresh start, and in the early 2000s, he moved to Deckers. "When I got to Deckers, the company was doing about $200 million in revenue but there was not a lot of routine," explains Martinez.

Turning the Ship around

Harkening back to skills he developed in his teenage years, running mile after mile between jobs, Martinez helped rebuild his organization from the ground up, streamlining policies and procedures for the organization to follow. "It would be ludicrous to suggest one person can change a company all by himself," says Martinez. "We did it together. Still, the first element of leadership is pulling everyone together for a common purpose and mission. We generated a stable environment, a bubble in which to thrive." Modesty aside, the results of Martinez's actions speak to what he did. Like the behind-the-scenes structural support that Bickford and Klapow provided their organizations, Martinez brought balance and equilibrium to Deckers, taking the company to $1.8 million in ten years.

The Takeaway

Without a doubt, these three examples of high performers in various industries: art, sports, and business, represent the summit of what's humanly possible. In each instance, we viewed achievers struggling against the very limits of their craft and even survival itself. Through these firsthand accounts, we also witnessed the types of exemplary achievements that can be obtained with strict discipline and a will to control one's own time.

The fact is, humans are the only species capable of not only changing themselves from the inside—but transforming their outside environment. And as we have just seen, true alchemy on an almost superhuman level can and does occur when we accept this premise: we can for a time create and live in our own bubble. Safely ensconced in our temporary world, we have the power to dream anew, creating visions of greatness. Now, let's consider what to do when it becomes clear that our time bubble is no longer cutting it.

CHAPTER 8

When Your Bubble Goes Pop

ON PAPER, MAX HAWKINS'S LIFE COULDN'T HAVE BEEN BETTER. The twenty-eight-year-old software engineer had tons of friends and a cushy job at Google. Forget about inhaling a quick cup of joe before braving San Francisco's horrific traffic. Instead, on the daily, he eased into his morning with five-star artisanal coffee before enjoying a pleasant bike ride to the company campus.

Still, ever the systems thinker, Hawkins worked on concocting ways to refine his life, beginning with his commute. "I optimized my schedule to be perfect," he tells me in an interview. "I was constantly shaving one or two seconds, making it slightly faster so I could get into work faster."

When he did roll into the office, life continued unfolding sweetly. Not only did he relish the engineering tasks he was assigned, but he was also able to devote up to 20 percent of his time to meaningful projects. Oh, and did I mention the food? Every day, Hawkins could count on enjoying regular perks, like complimentary epicurean delicacies prepared by Google's chefs. He might dine on lobster for lunch followed by Ben & Jerry's Phish Food-inspired cupcakes filled with marshmallows and topped with salted caramel buttercream.

His social life hummed along, too. He developed many meaningful relationships with his coworkers. Like him, they were young, outgoing, and successful. In between shifts, they would take advantage of premium Google amenities, like the rock-climbing wall and the volleyball court. In the evenings, he and his circle made the rounds at cool bars offering handcrafted cocktails.

Clearly, for all intents and purposes, Hawkins was killing it, living the dream of twenty-first-century urban millennials.

He had it all. And yet something felt wrong.

"When I was in high school, I wanted to work at a tech company in San Francisco building new software," says Hawkins. "That was always my aspiration. But when I arrived there, I realized it wasn't superfulfilling for me. My time bubble wasn't working. I had gotten to a place where I stopped learning. I was doing the things I thought I wanted to do, but found I was doing the same things repeatedly. I needed to go in a different direction."

In the last chapter we looked at high performers who reached the apex of their profession through designing and following routines of high precision and rigor. In the cases of the Rolling Stones and Jeff Gordon we observed how controlling their environment down to the minutest details helped them focus on their respective crafts. Likewise, we saw how CEO Angel Martinez transcended his circumstances by building a career around the stability a strong emphasis on routine affords.

Throughout this book we have argued that contrary to conventional wisdom, living in a bubble provides us with meaning, purpose, and joy. But like it or not, internal and external forces can pop our bubbles. These disruptive events often serve as a wake-up call. They challenge us to go within to restore normalcy, then develop new modes of being and doing to bring us the stability we crave.

Hawkins's story offers an illustration of what can happen when someone comes to the realization that their bubble is no longer working. Examining what he did to shake up his life offers important clues, especially for anyone who feels they are in a rut.

When the Blush Comes Off the Rose

Hawkins loved living in San Francisco. He loved his job. He loved his social network. He especially loved how every part of his life seemed tailored to his interests, until he read a paper on algorithms one day and realized he was living in his own algorithm. "I was at work when I happened to come across an academic piece on predictive analytics. The gist of it was that if you take data—for instance, someone's GPS trace—and fed it into an algorithm, you could predict with high certainty where they might be on a given day."

Often decried as invasive by data privacy critics, what Max is describing has become commonplace among smartphone users. If you've ever noticed Google Maps suggesting directions home at the time you usually leave work, this is an instance of machine-learning behavioral analytics. While such technological abilities may be viewed as a good thing, especially as a time saver, Hawkins thought differently.

The next day, Hawkins and his friend had plans to go out after work so he went on Yelp where he learned of a new bar. Again, on paper, it looked great. Hip. The kind of trendy place he so often went with buddies. "I thought of trying it out, but then stopped. I remembered that algorithm paper and it hit me. Isn't this bar exactly the type of place an AI might guess I would go based upon my past choices?"

We Are the Choices We Make

The celebrated artist James Joyce who wrote psychological novels like *Dubliners* and *Ulysses* is also renowned for extolling the importance of the "epiphany" which has been described as a sudden burst of knowledge shining light on something previously hidden. Put simply, epiphanies are "eureka" moments. They shake us from complacency, awakening us to deeper truths.

At this moment—right before he was about to grab a drink with his friend—Hawkins experienced his own epiphany, one that would cast doubt on the time bubble he had so meticulously constructed. "Where was *I* in all this?" he asked himself at that moment. "I realized I wasn't really in control at any point in the chain of my life. Each event was a consequence of the previous. It was all so *automatic*."

While Hawkins took responsibility for his past choices, he couldn't help thinking there must be a way to escape the cage he had built. He also wondered how a computer could know so much about him to even predict a new bar he might deign to visit. Or as he says, "Had I become so . . . so predictable?" Of course, predictability isn't entirely bad. As the COVID-19 panic proved all too well, when we go to the grocery store, we want reassurance that we will find the items we need to feed ourselves (and that the shelves won't be empty). Likewise, when we visit the doctor, we want this person to follow predictable protocols concerning hygiene and due diligence.

Yet, when it comes to designing a life filled with wonder and delight, predictability can be a hindrance. So far, we have discussed the benefits of routine in the service of certainty. Without a doubt, exacting time bubbles such as the one Hawkins fashioned for himself can provide needed stability, a requisite for living longer, managing travel, and developing high performance. Yet, we owe it to ourselves to ask what we should do when our bubbles no longer serve us. Or as another celebrated novelist, Paulo Coelho, puts it in starker terms: "If you think adventure is dangerous, try routine. It's lethal."

Routine Hacking

Coelho's words—or at least the spirit they convey—must have been swimming in Hawkins's conflicted mind when he decided to use his software skills to engineer his way out of his problem. Committed to breaking the dull trajectory his life had taken, he created an app integrating with Uber. "Randomness was key," Hawkins explains. "To get out of my own way I had to disrupt the tendency of my choices to follow a predictable pattern."

Like how double-blind testing works to eliminate bias, Hawkins removed his preferences from the equation. "Paradoxically, the way out of my routine rut was to have an even stricter routine. I also discovered there's actually more freedom in turning over some of your will to a process outside of yourself. The problem with my old routine was I was doing the thing that seemed obvious to do next. To break that, I had to stick to a strict routine determined by something outside of myself: a randomized computer algorithm."

As mentioned, Hawkins was living an existence governed by aligning his interests. To escape the potential to influence his future decisions, he effaced his preferences from the process of ride sharing. "Most of us are used to telling Uber where we want to go," says Hawkins. "But I disabled that function. There was no way for me to select a drop-off location. Instead, the app chose a place for me to go and a car took me there. Afterward, I was on my own to experience whatever came next."

What came next was quite different from what happened before. Instead of journeying to the trendy bar he found on Yelp, Hawkins and his friend let the app randomly pick their destination that night. This choice led them to a part of town they hadn't been before. Only, when they got there, they thought there must be some mistake. The sign outside the building said: San Francisco Psychiatric Emergency Center. Hawkins laughs about this now. "In hindsight, this was pretty appropriate. But at least I was getting outside of my shell."

Galvanized that the app worked—even if its first suggestion was a dud, Max doubled down on his experiment. "I was hooked," he says. In the months to come, he abdicated responsibility for the content of his bubble to more randomness. He let his app decide what he should do in his free time. This decision—to non-decide— led Hawkins to random new hair salons, florists, museums, bowling alleys (and, yes, bars). Hawkins loved the results his random generating app was suggesting. For the first time in a while, life was novel and fun again.

But he didn't stop there. Hawkins began randomizing in other ways. "I did a bunch of experiments where I applied this idea to other areas where I realized there was a stagnant pattern." He began building randomized schedules. For instance, he made a list of all of the things he did during the day and then had the computer assign them different time windows. He tried out this new schedule to see how it changed things, even going so far as to allow the computer to suggest sleep schedules. "It had me napping for fifteen-minute intervals throughout the day which ended up being unsustainable."

Hawkins only put up with such drastic content tweaks for about a week or so because of their intensity, but he at least found the foray illuminating in that it showed crucial ways his old routine had shaped his behavior. More importantly, this experiment shook up his world—in a good way.

Eager to go further, he wondered how else he could apply randomness to his bubble. He soon let the computer decide in what part of the world he should live. This decision sent him all over: Essen, Germany; Gortina, Slovenia; Taipei, Taiwan; Mumbai, India. And each time Hawkins moved to a new city he kept up his random generator app, allowing it to determine what he would do and where he would go.

Just like in San Francisco, Hawkins's bubble now included new content, challenging old beliefs, forcing him out of his comfort zone. For instance, though he doesn't consider himself flexible, he made himself attend numerous yoga classes, including something called acroyoga (acrobatics plus yoga). Adamant to not let his preferences get in the way, he let the app expose him to networking socials, chess matches, community center pancake breakfasts, and even private events where he wasn't invited.

Of course, Hawkins is savvy enough to realize that his choice to live so boldly might not be possible without the privileges his revenue, race, and gender enable. Yet, he's also sensitive to the fact that escaping his humdrum existence brought him new insights. "What I realized through this experiment was that oftentimes the things you might enjoy are much larger than you'd think. People get trapped in a small sense of self. As a result, they don't allow themselves to be exposed to different ways of being."

To illustrate, Hawkins offers the example of music. "Before I did this experiment, I thought I knew what music I liked. That Kendrick Lamar was the best rapper and so on. Then I randomized my musical taste by choosing unusual songs on Spotify. I discovered I actually love classical music and certain country artists. I had been limiting myself by not allowing myself to experience new things I might enjoy."

Further Implications

Beyond expanding our sense of self and our musical horizons, Hawkins's experiment offers wisdom in the age of ever more sophisticated algorithms. To understand why, we must go back in time. In 1948, the behavioral psychologist B. F. Skinner published the novel *Walden Two*. At its core, the story concerned attempts to alter people's behavior to build a utopia. Back then, Skinner's ideas were greeted with harsh criticism. Academics especially took special aim at him for trying to control people via top-down social planning.

Flash-forward a few decades and suddenly Skinner's ideas are in fashion, though now known as applied behavior analysis and brought to us by what Harvard researcher Shoshana Zuboff calls surveillance capitalists. In her 2019 book, *The Age of Surveillance Capitalism: The Fight for a Human Future at the New Frontier of Power*, Zuboff makes the case that the big tech giants of the world—Google, Facebook, Amazon, etc. profit from an asymmetry of power.

According to Zuboff, these multinationals earn big revenues by misappropriating our data to not just help advertisers sell us things, but also by nudging us toward actions that will serve their interests. As Katie Fitzpatrick writes for the *Nation*, "Silicon Valley firms don't want to simply monitor our behavior, however; they plan to shape it, too. By integrating these devices into our daily lives, these companies also set the stage for a future of more direct intervention."

As someone who has spent much time working for Google and is aware of this phenomenon, Hawkins cautions us to beware the many (unnoticed) algorithms subtly nudging us toward routines serving others' commercial interests. "I'm critical of many AI applications because they're usually built by corporations with an incentive to change our behavior in a way that might not be beneficial for us. The person who's paying Facebook is the advertiser, not you. Together, they work opaquely to manipulate your behavior."

To this point, Hawkins makes it clear in his recent TED Talks that his decision to randomize his life wasn't just due to his own disillusionment. He fears corporate influence in the AI age and urges resistance. "There are many questions about the ways in which these algorithms are controlling our lives," he says on stage. "If you just do the default—if you follow your preference and go in the direction that everything else is going, it's really easy to be caught in a place where you can be controlled."

When Change Comes from the Outside

Now, let's shift gears to discuss what happens when external circumstances disrupt our lives. COVID-19 couldn't provide a more apt example of this phenomenon. Drummer Evan Howard is a band leader for a jazz group based in New York City. Prior to March 2020 he could count on dozens of monthly gigs, not just in the tristate area, but also in international locales, from the Caribbean to the United Kingdom.

Then the pandemic struck. Not only did all of his band's scheduled performances evaporate, but he also found himself quarantined to his Brooklyn apartment with his girlfriend who had only made the leap to move in with him a month prior. "Luckily, it turns out we are really compatible," says Howard, who is happy to report they quickly found a way to optimize their routines so they didn't drive each other crazy, but instead, fell deeper in love.

In addition to crises outside our control, such as the pandemic and its economic fallout, our very nature can act as an external force, shaking up our reality. Let me explain. At the beginning of this book, we discussed how the womb constitutes our first experience of the time bubble. As we are born and grow, our worldview increases. The content of our bubbles becomes ever more complex but for years it feels like life is proceeding on an even keel.

Then puberty hits. "Sure, most of us know the telltale signs of puberty—hair growth in new places, menstruation, body odor, lower voice in boys, breast growth in girls, etc.," writes Steven Dowshen, MD, for KidsHealth.Org. But physical transformations aside, a psychological disruption is also at play.

Hormonal upheavals, not to mention new societal expectations, can't help but herald a vastly different existence for boys and girls in this chaotic phase. "Put simply, during this time, children begin to naturally pull away from their families and connect with their peers to establish independence and individuality," writes Lauren DiMaria for VeryWellMind.com. As a result (and as any parent of a teen well knows), children going through puberty are prone to moodiness, anxiety—not to mention depression.

On the other side of the age continuum is the chaos caused by menopause. Demarcating the end of the menstrual cycle, it usually occurs after a woman has gone a year without a period. Like puberty, menopause is a natural biological phase. However, it can be just as disruptive on both the body and mind.

When it comes to the former, menopause's arrival coincides with physical occurrences, like hot flashes, irritability, and sleep disturbances. These symptoms can lead to anxiety, but there is another reason this life stage wreaks havoc. Many women experiencing menopause happen to be of the age in which major familial transitions are also occurring, resulting in a double whammy.

The NIH's National Institute on Aging resource helps shed light on this phenomenon with the following case study: "Larissa is fifty-two. She's excited for when her children leave home, and she has more time for her other interests. She's looking forward to traveling and taking a computer class. But recent health changes have been getting in the way of her plans."

As humans live longer, more outside pressures threaten to shatter the stability of long-held time bubbles. "Over the past twenty years, the divorce rate in the United States has actually declined," writes divorce mediator Joe Dillon for EquitableMediation.com. "But for the over-fifties, the divorce rate has actually doubled." Beginning in 2004, such marital dissolutions began to be known as gray divorces. Writing for *Forbes*, wealth advisor Marguerita Chang points to key factors influencing the influx of breakups among the older population, including addiction, financial management, and infidelity.

However, the underlying issue Chang points to has a psychological basis. "Life spans have drastically increased, and even at age fifty or above people think they have time to discover what makes them happy in marriage," she writes. "Older people have stopped shying away from the idea of divorce after drifting away from their partners because they still believe they can find happiness."

Like Hawkins's internal desire to change, it is becoming increasingly common that one spouse has had enough of the other and starts divorce proceedings, even at an age in which many are contemplating retirement. This decision to separate can deal a blow to the spouse who might otherwise be happy keeping their bubble as is. (Sidenote: Divorce rates exploded throughout China in the wake of COVID-19 after the quarantine was lifted. "The city of Xian, in central China, and Dazhou, in Sichuan province, both reported record-high numbers of divorce filings in early March, leading to long backlogs at government offices," writes Sharidon Prasso for *Bloomberg Businessweek*. "In Hunan province's Miluo, 'staff members didn't even have time to drink water' because so many couples lined up to file, according to a report in mid-March on the city government website. Clerks struggled to keep up, processing a record number in a single day, it said.")

Another prime disruptor impacting the elderly's routine concerns a challenge affecting more and more families: relocation. But first, to put the problem in context, we now turn to columnists Andrew Stein and Mark Penn writing for the *Hill*. "As a nation, we are totally unprepared for what is happening. By 2050, the population of people over the age of 65 will nearly double, from 47.8 million to 88 million, and 10 million of them will be over age 90."

As seniors advance to an age in which they can no longer care for themselves, we will see a huge uptick in elderly living in care facilities. As previously mentioned, the chaos this will unleash for both the aged and their loved ones cannot be overstated. Writing for *Express*, columnist Will Stone says that moving to a new home is "more stressful than a relationship breakdown, divorce, or even a new job, according to research."

It is little wonder that authors Marie Reidl and Franco Mantovan found that being in a nursing home can have deleterious impacts on an individual's identity. Offering the results of their study in the journal *Hindawi*, they categorize the damage in this manner. "The change in social status, the impact on autonomy, the feeling of having no place to call home, the change in social contacts, and the reduction of habitual activities rank first in the presentation of the results and endanger the people's identity which they had before."

Rebuilding Our Time Bubble

Certainly, there are many other harrowing external forces that can disrupt the most solid of routines. These include but aren't limited to job loss, sickness, and the death of a loved one. Still, no matter what we are up against, we must push on. How we are wired forces us to recreate stable structures despite destructive forces beyond our control.

Now that we have discussed some of these challenges, let's look at how we can rebuild our bubbles. Returning to the subject of divorce, I wish to share with you a story about one of my coauthors who experienced such disruption.

His narrative will inform the eleven steps I encourage pursuing to rebuild one's bubble whenever a traumatic event throws us for a loop. (Important caveat: These steps are but a suggestion. Everyone's situation is unique and therefore requires discernment to determine the best course of action.)

That said, let us turn our attention to Joe Garner.

Joe's Divorce

After nearly nineteen years of marriage, Joe's wife decided she wanted to "be on her own for a while," leaving him alone with their nine-year-old daughter and fifteen-year-old son. Joe was determined to do everything he could to keep his children's bubble intact. As a result, he put his focus on making sure they stuck to their former routines despite the profound disruption.

To do so, he set up an emergency/interim bubble to keep things as normal as possible. He reestablished a healthy regimen first (knowing the mind would follow later). This meant sticking to their home and school activities, including well-rounded meals. To better facilitate the transition, he also made sure to wake early to prepare a healthy breakfast timed to the kids' schedule. Meanwhile, he kept the table conversation positive, fun, and future-focused.

Despite these new difficulties, Joe could at least count on good role models who taught him how to persevere in hard times. "I was a lucky child," Joe says. "I grew up in a household where the power of positive thinking was preached routinely." During this transition, Joe often channeled his parents to keep up the forward momentum.

At the same time, he created a new bubble informing his kids' physical and social life, ensuring he was there to fill in any needed gaps between their old existence and their new. As a test to see if this new mode of being and doing was working, Joe likes to tell the following anecdote:

> *My children were enrolled in Catholic schools and one of our routines was attending the Sunday morning mass. One Sunday, the priest asked the kids to sit at the altar as he began his homily.*
>
> *He asked them, "Where is your favorite place and why?"*
>
> *Hands shot in the air, including my daughter's. One little boy said he loved Magic Mountain because of the roller coasters. Another little girl said she loved going to her grandmother's because she always had fresh baked cookies. Meanwhile, my daughter was still waving her hand, but was never called on. Frankly, I was relieved because I had no idea what she would say.*
>
> *When she got back to the pew, I asked her, "Sweetie, if Father had called on you, what were you going to say? Where's your favorite place?"*
>
> *"Home," she replied.*
>
> *"Why?" I asked.*
>
> *"Because that's where I feel loved and safe."*
>
> *My bubble was intact.*

One final word about Joe's transition. Early on, he would often reach out to his children's teachers and the parents of his kids' friends asking them to share anything that could possibly be of concern. This small act allowed him to constantly tweak their bubble as needed—in real time.

The Art of the Time Bubble

As discussed, we live from womb to tomb in a succession of time bubbles. Often, these are disrupted in our journeys. Whenever this occurs, we are tasked with creating a new bubble. These bubbles may be thought of as an art form, a creative process informed by how we are wired as well as the science governing our species and its social structures.

So, how do we go about creating and recreating optimal time bubbles? And how do we choose environments best suited to help us thrive and give our days meaning? Insights on these questions may be found in the stories throughout this book. But to deal with the challenge of this chapter, the one which Joe faced—what to do when our bubble pops—we may consult the following steps.

1. **Recognize** when an inciting event or incident is causing instability.
   Joe's separation from his wife.
2. **Become** aware that the time bubble has burst.
   Joe's recognition that his old way of life was no more.
3. **Minimize** the duress, stress, and disruption.
   Joe did everything in his power to keep things normal for his children.
4. **Begin** an emergency/interim time bubble.
   Joe took steps to establish the basis of a substitute routine.
5. **Gain** clarity and perspective on the past and future.
   Joe visualized the new life he wished to create with his kids.

6. **Establish** healthy priorities around diet, exercise, and sleep.
   Joe kept up the old structure of mealtimes and rest to maintain his children's stability.
7. **Ruminate** on the past and contemplate the future.
   Joe kept his eye on what was coming to stave off any dangers.
8. **Create** a new physical and social bubble.
   Joe designed a mental plan and visualized how he would implement it.
9. **Execute** regularity in the bubble.
   Joe embarked on a new routine offering his kids needed stability.
10. **Test** for meaning and purpose.
    Joe continually watched his children to ensure they continued to function well in their new circumstances.
11. **Refine** and improve continuously.
    Joe never stopped working on ways to better his family's situation through constant vigilance.

Now that we have explored ways to manage and adapt when our bubble goes pop, it is time to enlarge our conversation to the collective. In the next chapter we will look at how businesses can maintain and recreate their bubbles, even when crisis threatens an organization's livelihood and stability.

CHAPTER 9
There's Nothing Routine about a Company Crisis . . . or Is There?

JUST BEFORE 6:00 A.M., Megan Sullivan appeared at the bus stop for her ride to City College. An urgent need to perform well on her final exam, coupled with hours of cramming, had made it hard for the eighteen-year-old nursing student to get much sleep the night before. A thoughtful person, Megan had learned firsthand how to care for others in high school when her father was diagnosed with cancer. While her peers were busy Snapchatting or worrying about prom, Megan spent every waking minute caring for her dad beside her mother.

Unfortunately, their efforts were not enough. Not that it was their fault. Even his A-team of doctors confessed there was little they could do. They caught the cancer too late. The best her father could hope for was loving care during his remaining time. This, Megan freely gave him. And when he finally passed in the early morning hours, she made a silent vow that her mission in life would be to care for others—to see that they, too, were lovingly seen and attended to—no matter their chances of survival.

Now, less than five years later, Megan found herself at a critical juncture once again in the early morning hours. As soon as she boarded the bus, it would take her to school where she would face her crucial exam. If she did well, she would be admitted to nursing school to realize her dream.

All that mattered now was that she keep her mind clear. She must remember all those facts she wrote in her notes. *Breathe*, she told herself. *Just breathe and everything will turn out fine.*

The moment her bus rounded the corner, Megan inched forward with a smile of determination. She never saw the car coming. Before Megan could take another breath, the man at the wheel lost control, plowing straight into her.

* * *

Paramedics rushed to the grisly scene to find an unconscious young woman on the pavement. Severe trauma had damaged her lower extremities, abdomen, and chest. She was barely alive and covered in blood. Quickly, the medics transported her to the nearest emergency room. When her gurney burst through the doors of Trauma Room 1, the assembled team was ready to put to work their years of experience and diagnostic skills.

Only not everyone was on board with the mission.

"Ugh. Another drunk driver?" said the trauma surgeon as he entered. He pointed to Megan while washing his hands. "And who's this?"

Before anyone could respond, he answered his own question. "I know. Someone who ought to be home this early. Instead of dragging me out of bed."

Before he could don his sterile gloves, the most experienced ER nurse—a middle-aged woman who had seen a lifetime of misery—grabbed him by the scrubs and pulled him aside.

She whispered, "Do your job. Lead this team. But respect everyone." Then she added, "I am here doing just that—trying to save my daughter."

* * *

What I just shared is a true story, though I changed the name of the woman involved and modified details so as not to implicate anyone. Sadly, this is not an isolated incident. It's becoming ever more common in our less than civil society. But before we discuss the lesson here, I would like to back up to discuss the focus of this chapter.

We are nearly at the end of this book. From the outset, I have made the case that humans, like all earthly organisms, are governed by chronobiological factors. This means that we are wired to respond to solar- and lunar-related rhythms, both consciously and unconsciously. Since the dawn of mankind, we have risen with the sun and fallen asleep at night. Even in smog-covered cities, in which it's impossible to see the heavens, our bodies still sync to the natural fluctuations of time.

Time's importance, reflected in the concept of the time bubble, cannot be overstated. From womb to tomb, we structure our days with specific content informing our values and generating our identity. Chapter after chapter we looked at how we can alter our environment and vary our behavior to achieve different outcomes. Yet, at our core, humans are driven by the need for stability and certainty.

This is the core of routine and why its practice is central to a well-lived existence. Now, I wish to focus on how routine may be used in the service of business. Specifically, let's delve into how organizations can stave off the worst exigencies of crisis by adhering to three principles closely aligned with the major themes of this book.

These concepts are not meant to be mere hypotheticals or armchair musings. Rather, they compose insights gleaned from my c-suite tenure. As a former emergency physician turned CEO of a multimillion-dollar emergency medical care organization, I have learned much about maintaining balance amid upheaval. As it turns out, the corporate realm isn't so different from the ER. Investment in structures and a commitment to balance can keep companies from the brink, whether it be a devastating lawsuit, the travails of bankruptcy, or even a pandemic. As professionals, we really *can* prepare for the chaotic and unexpected.

So, without further ado, let's dive into the ways in which incorporating routine into business culture can stave off the worst crises and dangers.

Insight 1: Insist on Decorum and Mutual Respect

The story of Megan Sullivan is unfortunately all too common. Way before the Me Too movement revealed workplace toxicity to be festering at a staggering level, civility has been under attack. Writing for Business.com in 2017, columnist Stuart Hearn cited a study by Clear Review indicating that 40 percent of employees say they don't feel appreciated. "Do you get the impression that your employees are increasingly disgruntled, disengaged, and frustrated with their roles, or even your company in general?" he asks.

It's a question worth asking, especially if you are a business leader tasked with providing a work atmosphere conducive to success. After all, there are demonstrable signs that social media and our "cancel culture" are undermining etiquette and politeness.

For those who may be unaware of cancel culture or how it is leading to negativity, we would do well to consult Aja Romano. Writing for *Vox* in 2019 and citing celebrities such as Kanye West, Scarlett Johansson, Gina Rodriguez, and Kevin Hart as individuals who have received such societal backlash, he describes this phenomenon as the idea someone can be canceled—or prevented from having a popular platform—based on their words or deeds.

"Within the past five years, the rise of 'cancel culture' and the idea of canceling someone have become polarizing topics of debate as a familiar pattern has emerged: A celebrity or other public figure does or says something offensive," he writes. "A public backlash, often fueled by politically progressive social media, ensues. Then come the calls to cancel the person—that is, to effectively end their career or revoke their cultural cachet, whether through boycotts of their work or disciplinary action from an employer."

Understandably, there are instances in which deplorable behavior should be rightfully condemned by society. However, what is concerning is how meme culture, cyberbullying, and the preponderance of online trolling have reduced our capacity to empathize with one another. It is important that we as a people observe norms of civility, especially in times of crisis. Whether it be caring for a person suffering from a critical injury or attempting to save a company in the throes of a death spiral, our go-to mode of being—our default routine—should be to focus on the mission while respecting others.

And yet, respect for others can often be the first thing that disappears in times of stress. It's not hard to see why. When the brain is in the grip of fight or flight, we can slip into survival mode. We can become egocentric, incapable of compassion or empathy. But this is exactly the wrong way to behave in a crisis. The best leaders know you can calm everyone in the room *and* increase team spirit by working as a group instead of as individuals. Likewise, the more you can keep the bigger picture in mind instead of getting lost in detail, the more focused the group will remain on the task at hand.

Certainly, there will be times when it seems preferable to cast blame on one person for the good of the group, but we should avoid this route. We need look no further than the actions of China's leader Xi Jinping during the coronavirus outbreak to observe the bankruptcy of this approach. Instead of taking responsibility for the secrecy that prevented authorities from responding more swiftly to the crisis, he shifted blame to local communist officials. "I issued demands during a Politburo Standing Committee meeting on January 7 for work to contain the outbreak," Jinping was quoted in February 2020 by the *Washington Examiner*. "[We must] inform the people of what the party and government is doing and what is our next step forward to strengthen the public's confidence."

As a point of comparison, we may contrast these statements placing blame on others to the capable way Starbucks CEO Kevin Johnson handled a public relations fiasco that could have easily engulfed his company. In 2018, two African American men were arrested at a Philadelphia Starbucks because the manager said they didn't purchase beverages. When news of this event broke, it unleashed a torrent of public anger at the men's mistreatment.

Instead of throwing the manager under the bus, Johnson rushed to emphasize Starbucks' *shared* values of responsibility and accountability. Recognizing the need for mutual respect, he also issued a public apology on behalf of the organization. Again, rather than shifting blame to some lone bad apple, he instituted a culture of responsibility replete with seminars for the collective to standardize routine practices for equitable treatment.

As a result of these quick and decisive actions on the part of Johnson, approximately 8,000 of the employees had a complete day off for training on what was called the new "third place policy." Talk about an inclusive culture. In the wake of the crisis, Starbucks doubled down on its dedication to an environment of civility for *all* guests—even those who haven't (yet) bought anything by making the following announcement: "We want our stores to be the third place, a warm and welcoming environment where customers can gather and connect. Any customer is welcome to use Starbucks spaces, including our restrooms, cafes, and patios, regardless of whether they make a purchase." (Sidenote: Starbucks' stock soared since the incident, reaching an all-time high close on July 26, 2019. Evidently, the company's practice of structured civility paid major dividends.)

Insight 2: Enforce a Distinct, Recognized Chain of Command

If you have ever witnessed a cardiac arrest or the sudden loss of consciousness, the adrenaline can be intense. When this happens, clear-headed thinking can go out the window, along with the ability to dispassionately assess the situation. Why? Again, most crises put people into fight-or-flight mode, eliminating the ability to think rationally. Worse, the problem can be compounded in a group setting where personalities and noise intensify responses.

This is just the challenge I faced when I encountered Robert one day in my old life as an ER physician. A true philanthropist, Robert had spent much of his time giving back to our local Catholic hospital which was staffed by nurses and nuns. Robert developed the first charitable golf tournament in the city and was even able to make it a success as a major event with golf professionals participating. Little did Robert dream the same hospital he spent his life supporting was where he would end up dying from a heart attack.

It just so happens I was the person asked to go to Robert's room to pronounce him dead. Upon entering, I noticed a group of family members and sisters holding space. They were quiet, appreciating the gravity of this solemn moment, assured in the knowledge that death was soon to come.

Then I noticed something. There was but one voice speaking. It was a sister, quietly praying, leading everyone. Despite seeing so many faces filled with tears, I couldn't help noticing how peaceful it felt here. Everyone was being comforted and comforting others. I was in the midst of paying my respects to Robert's wife when suddenly Code Blue rang out in room 201 on the floor above.

Someone else was going into cardiac arrest.

Quickly, I sprang into action. Running up the stairs to the room, I found a middle-aged man unconscious. Beside him were responding nurses with their cardiac cart and defibrillator at the ready. However, unlike the scene on the floor beneath me, pandemonium had gripped this room. A riot of noise and movement had nurses and nuns scrambling with no authority in charge. Taking a page out of the sister's playbook, I determined to bring order to the chaos, beginning with the way I spoke.

"Everyone, slow down," I said. "Listen to my voice and only my voice."

Recognizing the need for organization, I subdued the panic by being organized and steadfast. Responding to my calm manner, the team of nuns and nurses transformed before my eyes. They began to move quietly and efficiently as I directed them to give me equipment for intubation. In seconds, we began an intravenous line to defibrillate the patient. With their help, I resuscitated the patient without further issue. That day, I learned that leading a team in a time of crisis requires the same measured approach as the reverence of a single voice praying.

* * *

Based on the previous insight, it must seem anathema to suggest employing a chain of command when crisis strikes, but this is just what is needed. Yes, it is important to value group effort, especially in leading an organization toward its goal, but when the unexpected hits, someone must take charge. (In a respectful manner, of course.) One voice must rise above the chatter to deliver a targeted message in times of insanity. Order is *not* a democracy when things go to hell.

On the other hand, one of the greatest errors in judgment is to merely delegate to others in a catastrophe, hoping things will turn out fine. Just think about what might have happened in room 201 if I had allowed a committee to decide how best to defibrillate the dying patient. Unless a miracle occurred, the man would have likely died. Instead, on that day I took my cue from observing how the sister took charge of the room beneath me. Hers was a calming presence lighting the way for others, leading me to employ the same useful tactics.

To this point, problems can exacerbate when leaders don't say, "Hey, I'm in charge here. The buck stops with me." Of course, perceived authoritarianism may be unwelcomed in less challenging times, but it's key to instilling stability when an individual—or organization—is under attack. This notion of a central command in times of crisis takes on new levels of importance when the business challenge in question is public facing. Dr. W. Timothy Coombs, writing for the Institute for Public Relations in a 2014 article entitled "Crisis Management and Communications" had this to say on the subject: "From a public relations perspective, this take-control approach by senior leadership to quickly acknowledge the problem and explain what is being done to correct the issue, reassures the public and imbues a certain level of confidence in the senior leadership of the company."

Too often, however, leadership fails to provide a unified front, especially when facing a PR crisis. We can see this vividly illustrated in United Airlines' mishandling of a recent situation that need not have gone so wrong. On April 8, 2018, crew members asked passengers on a Louisville, Kentucky-bound United flight 3411 at Chicago O'Hare International Airport to voluntarily give up their seats for compensation. Apparently, four of the crew were needed on the flight to work another in Louisville to prevent a cancellation.

When sixty-nine-year-old Dr. David Dao Duy Anh, one of the passengers, refused to give up his seat because he had a patient he needed to see the next day, the Chicago Department of Aviation Security got involved. Officers forcibly removed him from the plane by striking Dao's face against the armrest and pulling his unconscious body across the aisle past rows of aghast passengers.

If this malfeasance had happened a couple of decades ago, perhaps United could have quietly slipped it under the rug. But this happened in the age of smartphones, so the fallout was huge. "On social media, the firestorm swept around the world," writes Julie Creswell and Sapna Maheshwari for the *New York Times*. "Chinese social media users accused United, which does a lot of business in the country, of racism by targeting Dr. Dao, who appeared to be Asian. In the United States, customers showed pictures of their United loyalty or credit cards cut into pieces. And lawmakers called for an investigation."

If that was bad, the fumbled reaction from United was worse. After the video went viral, United's CEO Oscar Munoz waited too long before issuing a statement in which he apologized for "re-accommodating" four passengers, including Dao. Sidestepping responsibility, he issued an internal memo blaming Dao as "disruptive and belligerent" that quickly leaked to the web.

As might be expected, Munoz's statements only inflamed critics who took aim at him for his insensitive and tone-deaf pronouncements. Meanwhile, his lack of coordination on a public stance led United to suffer a $1 billion market share loss on April 11, as Asian observers called for a boycott of a company they perceived as being racially biased. It got so bad that US legislators brought in executives from United and other airlines to testify on Capitol Hill on what were perceived to be abusive conduct toward passengers.

At the end of the day, it didn't have to be this way. Undoubtedly, United and other airlines have made mistakes like this in the past. Instead of flying by the seat of their pants (no pun intended), they could have established ongoing, company-wide standard operating procedures for potential crises to prevent such disaster, or at least mitigate the fallout.

What United's debacle shows us is that drawing from precedent gives us a context to work from. By establishing routine for the unexpected, future events don't have to feel so overwhelming. Nor do they have to go so badly. And, yes, in this instance, there *was* one voice speaking for the company—but this voice badly represented the organization. If a routine protocol had been established instead, including what to do and say in times of crisis, disaster could have been averted.

Insight 3: Remain Calm and Mindful No Matter What

Speaking of airplanes, some of us may have experienced the situation in which a flight attendant comes on the speaker to ask if a physician is on board. This happened to me once when it was late in the evening and a local thunderstorm had wreaked havoc on airline schedules. As might be expected, everyone who was delayed for hours and hours had grown weary from the "hurry up and wait" scenario. All around me, people were tired and cranky and just wanted to get home. (And I was one of them.)

Some five hours later, around 10:00 p.m., we received word that our Dallas flight would finally board for Los Angeles now that the inclement weather had passed. Tense and fed up, everyone hurried to board, pushing each other and exchanging less than pleasant words.

Entering the walkway, I noticed a man being loaded in a wheelchair looking ill, pale, and somewhat somnolent. I didn't think much of it as all around me people hustled to put their luggage in the overhead and find their seats. As we started to taxi across the runway, you could sense people breathing a sigh of relief. We were finally going to take off.

Then we stopped. The attendant came on the PA with a request that sent chills up my spine. "If there is a physician on board, please identify yourself . . ."

I waited for someone else to raise their hand but there were no takers.

After volunteering myself, a crew member asked me to assess the same man I had noticed in the wheelchair. He sat in the aisle seat near the middle of the plane with his head down. Fresh from vomiting, he complained of severe nausea.

As I observed him more, I could sense my fellow passengers staring at me with daggers in their eyes. They looked ready to tear me up if I said we needed to return to the terminal, delaying the flight even more.

And yet I knew this man's life depended on my objectivity. No matter what the (rightfully) upset passengers felt, I had a duty to remain calm and mindful, not reactive to a group who might just lynch me if I made an unfavorable decision.

As I internally debated what to do, I could feel sweat beading on my forehead. My blood pressure must have been sky high, matching my rapid breathing. Still, remembering my training, I made sure to take my own pulse, relax, and practice inhaling and exhaling in a controlled manner. Within a minute I was able to make the decision we could continue with the flight due to the stabilization of the man's condition.

While the crowd looked on, I gave him some of the anti-nausea medication I carried. Of course, concerns as to what could go wrong with the patient passed through my mind even after I returned to my seat. It was a three-hour flight and the sooner we could land the better.

After we were airborne, I continued to check on the passenger who slept most of the way. As I did, I practiced remaining calm and mindful. Fortunately, we landed without incident, and the passengers all applauded and thanked me. Two passengers even approached to tell me they were nurse practitioners.

"We're just glad you had to make that call," they told me. "And not us."

* * *

For a time, I managed a high-stress trauma unit dealing with emergencies far more extreme than the tense situation on that plane. Whenever I tell stories to friends about what we endured as a unit, I invariably receive the question, "But how did you keep your cool?" Some of them have even asked, "How did you keep your humanity?"

"By committing to the concept of triage," I would tell them. "Handle the most urgent concerns—the core problems—first. While remaining calm."

Triage matters so much because life can throw us problems that we don't think we can handle. This is especially true when it comes to business. For instance, back in my CEO days, I was heading up a company experiencing a bleeding of profits going into the third quarter. When it became evident that the organization was heading to the danger zone and that we might be out of business in weeks, we developed an operating procedure to fight this crisis—a new routine. We established a war room and went to the heart of the situation. In this case, collections. Doing so may be likened to a doctor checking for vitals. By zeroing in on the core issue—revenues—we pinpointed the most urgent matter and (calmly) fixed it.

The takeaway is that if and when calamity strikes, it does little good to be reactive. Reactive actions result from a place of fear and usually lack a broader understanding of what is at stake. By triaging in business, (i.e., focusing on what is most crucial, then handling the situation with mindfulness), you have a better shot at solving the problem.

However, acting from a place of mindfulness first can help in other ways. When I was on the plane and could feel the stares of my fellow passengers, I was susceptible to making a wrong decision due to the pressure. C-suite leaders will often find themselves in similar straits when it feels like the whole world is watching. And though I cannot be sure what Oscar Munoz felt during the United crisis, I imagine he entered panic mode.

This is not an ideal place from which to make decisions, especially vital ones affecting your company, employees, and customers. Why? New scientific findings have revealed that fight-or-flight stress inhibits our ability to think. Writing for *Psychology Today*, Relly Nadler, PsyD, MCC, cites research showing that anxiety can even temporarily lower our IQ scores, preventing us from thinking rationally. "The light goes out in the prefrontal cortex, which is our executive functioning and decision-making region of the brain."

As they say, knowledge is power, and it helps to know how the unexpected can impede our ability to think through any problem. Realizing how helpful it can be to pay attention to our own physiology when our stress levels rise is therefore the first step toward establishing a routine to prevent and/or mitigate disaster. When stress begins to mount, it's key that we take a moment to step away. Doing so might just enable us to address the issue objectively in the most detached manner. Only then do we have a real chance of restoring stability and staving off crisis.

Now that we are in the right headspace to contemplate . . . let us turn now to our final chapter on the future of decision-making, routine, and the time bubble in the age of AI.

CHAPTER 10

Thinking Machines and the Outsourced Time Bubble

MEET TWENTY-EIGHT-YEAR-OLD CAROLYN JENKINS. She believes in optimization. In making every nanosecond count. A time-management ninja, she can out-multitask the best lane-changing, thumb-texting NYC Uber driver. While others are busy listening to the trainer shouting commands in her spin class, Carolyn goes rogue. Switching her cordless earbuds to white noise, she uses her workouts to finish two books a week. After graduating summa cum laude in dual degrees, she became an associate at a Manhattan law firm, nailing partnership a month into year two.

Now, that's a lot of quantifiable data. Oh, and did I mention that Carolyn also likes to optimize her sex life? Recently, she signed up for Nice, an app monitoring sexual activity. It allows you to track your sexual encounters with a host of data, including when, where, how long, activities, and protection used. It even includes a section for custom notes. Not only that, but it also allows you to monitor your STD test dates to ensure you and your partner(s) stay healthy.

Sex apps like Nice are all about optimizing bedroom fun. It offers a user-friendly interface, allowing you to input your carnal info into a handy system composed of stars and sliders. Like all things tech—and nerdy—the benefit is in the data. You can assess your performance stats and amorous routine. Over time, you can even glean sex life patterns based on the prodigious records that Nice keeps. (FYI: If you're wondering, it seems to have no social networking features. Yet.)

The Age of the Quantified Self

Full disclosure: Carolyn is not a real person but rather a composite of personalities and attitudes. If she were alive today, Carolyn would be a member of the millennial generation. Sometimes dubbed "digital natives," this demographic differs from previous ones because its members grew up in a world where the Internet was a given. Unlike, say, boomers, millennials didn't have to learn how to use email or navigate social media halfway through life. Instead, they grew up tech-savvy with the "Internet in their pocket," confident in their ability to find any answer by Googling it.

It makes sense then that "Carolyn" and her IRL peers—men and women who grew up online, posting memes and swiping screens—would feel comfortable using tech for their most intimate activity. "Tech has become so ubiquitous and seamless in our lives," says actor and self-described champion of nerd culture himself, Wil Wheaton, in an article for the *New York Times*. "And because tech and personal tech and wearable tech are such a part of our daily existence, we want to know more about them."

Though not a millennial, Gary Wolf offers living proof of how wearable technology, coupled with big data, can be used in ever more intriguing ways for life optimization. One of the early writers for *Wired Magazine* and its former executive editor, he also founded the Quantifiable Self website, boasting this tagline: "Self-knowledge through numbers."

Wolf recently began his TED Talks by divulging some of the copious personal information his devices are busy collecting on him daily. "I got up this morning at 6:10 a.m. after going to bed at 12:45 a.m. I was awakened once during the night. My heartbeat was 61 beats per minute, my blood pressure 127 over 74. I had about 600 milligrams of caffeine, zero of alcohol. And my score on the Narcissism Personality Index, or the NPI-16, is a reassuring 0.31."

For more examples of the merits of quantified living for self-mastery—or at least self-improvement, let's consider Fitbit. Initially founded under the company name Healthy Metrics Research, Inc. in 2007, it has since become the third-largest wearable company in shipments, according to the International Data Corporation (IDC). Specializing in activity trackers and aided by wireless-enabled technology to optimize health, Fitbit measures the biometric data of its users, such as their heart rate, quality of sleep, and daily steps walked.

New Zealander Rachel W. (the name she goes by on the company's video) describes how using data-centric technology didn't just optimize her well-being, it saved her life. For years, she suffered from weight problems, exacerbated by Type II Diabetes. Worse, depression tormented her due to the fact she and her husband Mark wanted a child for years but couldn't conceive.

"We tried everything," says Rachel. "I was stunned by the lack of support I got. The attitude from doctors—from everybody— was that you're not going to fix it. You're just not going to get better. This is you, forever."

Over time, Rachel's depression worsened. She stopped talking to Mark. She stopped leaving the house. She couldn't even get out of bed most days. When she did, it was mostly to binge on junk food.

One day she hit rock bottom while looking in the mirror.

"I couldn't stop crying. I just cried and cried. I was crying so hard I literally thought I would choke to death."

Rachel says she knew she had to change. The one thing that made her feel better was walking. Bereft of any flesh and blood medical professional cheering her on, Rachel turned to the app on her wrist. Why? It didn't just provide biometric details. It offered her coaching and accountability. Something she wasn't getting anywhere in her life.

"My Fitbit guided me to keep increasing my steps. It motivated me to embrace doing 10,000 steps a day. None of this stuff happens by osmosis. You need to build on a goal, on a goal, on a goal—to get to where you're going."

As Rachel tells it, her 10,000 steps soon became 12,000 as she threw herself into a new fitness routine. She was only competing against herself, to improve herself. In three months, she lost 79 pounds and reconnected with Mark.

"I put diabetes behind me," she says between tears of joy. "And then I got pregnant. We were just amazed. There's not an option to give up—to go back. You need to find that purpose. That reason why. It changes everything."

From Data to Insight

Both Wolf's and Rachel's experiences offer something revelatory and topical. Throughout this book, we have discussed the need for routine; the fact that developing a time bubble—and living within it—can bring the body and mind the homeostasis they crave. All organisms on Earth strive for balance: to find food when hungry, warmth when cold, shelter from the elements. But as we have seen again and again, humans alone strive for something else: meaning and purpose.

Once more, we are reminded of philosopher Friedrich Nietzsche's quote, "He who has a *why* to live for can bear almost any *how*." What's different about today is that we need not depend on just our own minds to develop the best possible routine. We can outsource such decision-making to thinking machines.

Contrary to conventional wisdom, thinking machines are not forward-looking innovations. They are backward-looking, relying on previous data points to make patterns and inferences. But for years, key developments in AI stalled, stymied in large part due to the difficulties of processing and storing vast amounts of data.

All of this recently changed. "The convergence of several technology trends is accelerating progress," write the authors from the McKinsey Global Institute in a 2016 report entitled *The Age of Analytics: Competing in a Data-Driven World*. "The volume of data continues to double every three years as information pours in from digital platforms, wireless sensors, and billions of mobile phones. Data scientists now have unprecedented computing power at their disposal, and they are devising ever more sophisticated algorithms."

These sophisticated algorithms are responsible for upending our economy. First coined in 2013 by columnist David Brooks for the *New York Times*, the term Dataism is now often used to describe the emerging significance of big data on markets. "We've all heard about big oil," says Neil Sahota, an IBM master inventor who published *Own the A.I. Revolution: Unlock Your Artificial Intelligence Strategy to Disrupt Your Competition* with my coauthor Michael in 2019. "Everyone knows the twentieth century belonged to big oil. Look at all the wars fought to obtain the world's most precious commodity. But in the age of Google and the electronic car, when the biggest companies on the Nasdaq are in the information business, data is usurping oil's importance."

So, why is data important? From the micro to the macro, our world is made up of information. Computers demonstrate this fact to us every day. No matter the industry—aviation, restaurants, mercantile, apparel—computers drive business. Our power grids, streetlights—even our nuclear reactors and atomic weapons are managed by computers. And they do it all based on manipulating information, or more accurately, binary code. Believe it or not, every bit of information on this planet can be simplified and represented by a 1 or a 0.

It's therefore little wonder that in 2017, the *Economist* declared, "The world's most valuable resource is no longer oil but data." Of course, data has always been around. It just wasn't until recently that our technology reached the point where we could mine this resource economically. To understand this better, consider a 2013 article appearing in *AEIdeas*: "The cost per gigabyte of data storage provided by a USB flash drive has fallen from more than $8,000 when they were first introduced about ten years ago, to $.94 cents today."

This article appeared seven years ago. In the interim, not only has it gotten cheaper and easier to store data, it's cheaper and easier to *process* data. Think about it this way. The first computers used by NASA in the 1960s for guiding lunar landers onto the moon cost nearly $4 million apiece and were the size of a car. They were also restricted to only performing several hundred thousand operations per second. Their memory capped out in the megabyte range.

By way of contrast, the smartphone on your desk is millions of times more powerful than the Apollo 11 guidance computers.

Big Shifts Ahead

Based on these breakthroughs in data storage and processing power, our era has rightfully been termed the "Information Age." But what people don't realize is that we are on the verge of a paradigmatic shift in thinking on par with the Copernican Revolution. The way we make our most personal decisions—from our sexual partners, to our health choices, to our daily routines—is going to transform due to the falling cost of data storage and rising computing power.

As discussed, humans have shifted their beliefs toward authority at various times in the last few thousand years. Once upon a time, kings ruled us with "divine" authority. Later, we came to internalize decision-making as religion lost its sway and modern liberalist ideas swept the world. However, in the future, much of our choices regarding ritual and routine may be influenced or made for us through apps. To help contextualize this phenomenon, the *Guardian*'s Pamela Stephenson Connolly offers an equally valid rationale as to why more people like Rachel are fine with turning to their computers for help.

But first, let us recall that Rachel felt the medical community gave up on her. Or at least they weren't giving her the guidance she needed to get healthy. Her Fitbit, on the other hand, served as her de facto digital support system. Nonjudgmental, available 24/7, and endlessly patient, it guided her to health. Connolly, therefore, foresees AI acting in a kind of parental or mentorship role for people going forward. "Human beings need validation, and many seek it avidly. Our phones are beginning to take on the roles of conscience-surrogates, father-confessors, spokesmen for our prefrontal cortexes. We want their approval."

The historian and futurist Yuval Noah Harari agrees. He also predicts that we will become ever more comfortable relying on computers for advice in a recent interview for the *Atlantic*:

> Look at GPS applications, like Waze, and Google Maps.
> Five years ago, you went somewhere in your car or on foot.

You navigated based on your own knowledge and intuition. But today everybody is blindly following what Waze is telling them. That's not the most important example. But it is the direction we're talking about. You reach a juncture on the road, and you trust the algorithm. Maybe the juncture is to exercise, or maybe it's your career. Maybe it's the decision to get married. But you trust the algorithm rather than your own intuition.

Connolly and Harari are not alone in their assessment as to what's coming. The Head, Strategic Engagement Division at the United Nations' ITU, Frederic Werner, also believes we will soon outsource much of our decision-making to AI. "Even on matters as important as how we invest our personal finances, what we eat for dinner, and how we socialize, more and more, humans will consult their personal and biometric data to determine how to live."

To put Werner's words in context, consider the online dating site Match.com. It has more than 7.7 million paid users. The dating site eHarmony has 10 million. Both rely on algorithms rather than butterflies in the stomach to help users identify their future mate. So, why would people outsource their decision-making to these platforms? For one thing, we know ourselves to be fallible. And if we are honest, we might acknowledge that we don't know as much about ourselves as we think.

Data, on the other hand, doesn't lie. It never forgets. It's also impartial and quantifiable. Nonetheless, even if data is impartial, it doesn't mean the individuals or corporations controlling the AI-based algorithms don't have their own agendas. On page 109, we learned how Google employee Max Hawkins went so far as to randomize his life with an app to escape what he viewed as tyranny through corporate behavioral analytics. To reiterate, Max had grown alarmed by how he saw algorithms nudging him toward choices others wished him to make. As a result, he decided to regain control through popping his own time bubble.

Nonetheless, many businesses don't share the same feelings as Max about AI's growing influence on our daily lives. They see technology as a tool to be healthier than ever before. As a result, more startups are springing up to capitalize on biometric data usage to improve outcomes in other meaningful ways.

Zinx is one such company. Based in Spain, it is a fully integrated mobile health and wellness platform for social good built upon five key verticals: telemedicine, medical-grade devices, fitness, nutrition, and mental health. I spoke to Javier Oberoi, its cofounder, to learn more about how Zinx is using mobile solutions to help customers regain control over their health.

One such way is through the deployment of so-called smart sensors, such as a body analysis scale and an arm blood pressure monitor. Each can wirelessly connect and interact with an app to monitor biometric data. If the sensors detect a problem based on information received, they will alert the user and coordinate a teleconference between the person and a medical professional.

Oberoi's Zinx is one of a number of AI-empowered medical solutions seeking to democratize and decentralize today's flawed health-care system. Rather than requiring you to schedule an appointment with an overworked doctor, then wait in a lobby for hours only to see your caregiver for minutes, Zinx's products allow you to take a proactive role in monitoring your health, leading to greater wellness while reducing costs and wasted time.

An expert in the growing field of outsourced, user-controlled medicine via apps, Oberoi also indulged me to hypothesize what a routineology app for outsourced decision-making might be like. "As I'm sure you know, AI requires data to work," says Oberoi. "It thrives on information. If you want it to suggest the most optimal routines for users, I recommend affixing it to a smartwatch so it could learn about the person all day long. It could take biometric data, such as resting heart rate, blood pressure, and breathing rate as someone goes about their normal routine."

The Future of Decision-Making

For now, I have no plans to create my own routineology app. However, observing AI's growing efficacies for better health outcomes, I couldn't help wondering what an expert in the field might say about the future of decision-making in the Information Age. For this reason, I turned to Dr. Shahram Rahimi. Not only is he a professor and department head of computer science and engineering for Bagley College of Engineering, specializing in research concerning computational intelligence, machine learning, and predictive analytics, but he also serves on the board with me for the tech company Potentia Analytics.

Like Angel Martinez, Dr. Rahimi is a lifelong adherent and proponent of routine because his time bubble allowed him to escape his circumstances and build a successful career. Back in 1979, when he was nine years old, Dr. Rahimi's dad served as a high-ranking officer in the Iranian air force. He trained other pilots, including the son of Mohammed Reza Pahlavi, also known as the Shah. When the Iranian Revolution occurred that year leading to the Shah's defeat, Dr. Rahimi's father got kicked out of the military, decimating their family's stability.

"It was a challenging time for us, personally and as a country," Dr. Rahimi says. "You could not go 500 meters without being stopped three or four times by authorities who could question you on any pretense and lock you up." Just when the Rahimis thought things couldn't get worse, the Iran/Iraq war erupted in September 1980.

"The country was a mess and yet a very well-equipped Iraqi military needed to push forward. So, my father was called back into service."

As a ten-year-old kid, young Shahram found himself walking home every day from school praying his father hadn't been shot down or otherwise killed in the fighting. Meanwhile, a sustained bombing campaign from Iraq made it nearly impossible for him to stop the negative thoughts spiraling in his head. "It got so the only way for me to survive such a high level of stress was to put my focus on being the best at my school," says Dr. Rahimi. "I wanted to graduate, to go to the best universities. I wanted to be successful."

To accomplish his dream, Dr. Rahimi developed a time bubble, restoring needed stability to his life. "My routine was to wake up at 3:00 a.m. every day. Due to the frequent bombing, my family and I would all hunker down in the basement to be safer. We couldn't turn on the lights because they might draw attention to our house, so we used these heaters generating an orange light. For years, I would study by it. I studied every single day that way until it was time for breakfast and then off to school."

Dr. Rahimi's hard work paid off handsomely, allowing him to transcend his circumstances when the war ended and matriculate to the United States. Interestingly, he credits routine with also benefitting his little brother. "He's now a PhD in computer science and also a professor. Following my lead, he did the same thing, waking up early every day to bring needed order to his life. My little sister did it too. So, a strong routine can become contagious."

As we have seen, Dr. Rahimi's story, though harrowing, is not anomalous. Establishing a time bubble isn't just about determining the correct order of things one should do in a day. From analyzing the daily actions of top performers to observing how daily structure can restore hope to the hopeless, we have witnessed how powerful routine can be for (re)establishing purpose and meaning.

What's novel about Dr. Rahimi's work in AI is how computers can know us better than we know ourselves—and suggest ways to live better. "The benefit AI has over mankind is that when we process and evaluate data to learn from it, we have a limited view," Dr. Rahimi explains. "When it comes to considering the data, there is just too much for us to process. Humans are good at looking at a given problem, thinking about it, trying to solve it, then moving on to the next. But data science, specifically AI, can look at a much bigger picture, using more content and data as its basis."

When it comes to recognizing patterns informed by data, there is another way that AI could help *and* hinder humans. As we have discussed, the problem plaguing our species since the dawn of mankind has been uncertainty. To provide answers sorely lacking, communities and civilizations developed myths, rituals, and traditions to offer guidance, thereby establishing identity, group cohesion, and purpose.

Now, along comes AI and we are faced with an unusual prospect: the potential erasure of uncertainty. "Let us think about it this way," says Dr. Rahimi. "Suppose I earned an F in class because I put all the wrong answers on a test. I might learn my lesson from this failure—that is, if I am the kind of person who wishes to improve based on past mistakes. The iterative process of failing can lead to future success. This has been mankind's story for ages. But now, based on AI developments, it could be possible to one day remove failure altogether."

Dr. Rahimi's above scenario suggests a deep philosophical question we may one day face: Is it advisable to never be wrong again by relying on AI for the correct answer? Of course, this query presumes that AI would have all of the requisite data to be 100 percent accurate all of the time. For the sake of discussion, let's imagine this is possible. Where might such certainty lead us?

There are an infinite number of implications based on this scenario but let's ground our discussion to one. The German poet Christian Johann Heinrich Heine once said, "Experience is a good school. But the fees are high." If life were a novel, every person would be a dynamic character. As opposed to a static character, the former is an individual that changes over the course of the story due to their experiences. Essentially, our successes, but especially our failures, make us the people we are. Our mistakes, our foibles—our screwups—mold our personalities, for better or worse.

Now, if the emergence of omniscient AI were to somehow remove the need for us to ever make the wrong decision, what kind of people might we become? Though it's hard to predict what the future might hold under this hypothetical, it's my belief that we would be poorer as a species for not experiencing the personal and collective growth arising from uncertainty. Not only would we miss out on the chance to learn (even the hard way), but we would also open ourselves to untold problems should our computers suddenly stop working.

Ultimately, it's not easy to champion the need for such uncertainty, especially in a book about how routine can stave off chaos. And yet, I cannot endorse a future in which AI makes all our choices for us. (Even if it seems like it knows best.) Relying too heavily on a computer to plan one's life feels akin to cheating. After all, "Know thyself" is the commandment that Socrates, the Father of Philosophy, once promoted. If humanity's search for meaning comprises a never-ending struggle to gain knowledge and wisdom through experience and introspection, what would happen to us should we abdicate our duties to machines?

Yet, I can also see the allure of outsourced decision-making, especially in these uncertain times. "Man is born free, and everywhere he is in chains," begins the seminal book *The Social Contract* by Jean-Jacques Rousseau. "One man thinks himself the master of others but remains more of a slave than they are." Living in eighteenth-century Europe at the dawn of the Enlightenment, another age of uncertainty, Rousseau was appalled by the way he saw society corrupting the people around him. Rather than lifting humanity up, he viewed civilization as a destructive force denigrating the soul. Accordingly, he thought the original peoples of Earth had lived in an idyllic state of nature—that is, before modern life ruined everything.

Whether or not we believe Rousseau to be correct and that people would be better off away from big cities, skyscrapers, social media, and streaming television—not to mention smartphones that can analyze our biometrics to make life decisions for us—many would agree that modern life doesn't yet afford us the happiness and freedom we seek. Too often, burdened by responsibilities, jobs, health crises, and seemingly endless obligations, existence in the twenty-first century is far from a walk in the park, even for the most affluent.

Knowing that AI-enhanced apps are already optimizing and saving lives, is it really so bad to want our computers to generate better routines for us? To tell us how to live? After all, in my clinical practice, I saw so many patients dissatisfied by the ways their lives were going. They were lost, confused. Miserable.

Today, we need look no further than the opioid epidemic, the COVID-19 pandemic, or the staggering number of antidepressants prescribed to realize that many of us are hurting and dying. We feel alone and unmoored. However, even in these uncertain times, even when it feels like technological advances could release us from the pain we have grappled with for so long, I am not convinced we should do so. We must not abdicate our agency to thinking machines—even if they appear to know us better than we do ourselves.

Considering the choice we face as a species, I am reminded of the late poet Dylan Thomas's words, "Do not go gentle into that good night. Rage, rage against the dying of the light." Yes, instability and uncertainty continue to haunt us, wreaking havoc, causing endless distress and consternation. But like the ying belongs with its yang, like the sun needs its moon, we, too, are binary creatures. Our greatest strength lies in our greatest foe. As creatures wired by chronobiological rhythms of waxing and waning, coming and going, we will forever need problems to overcome and questions to answer. Practicing the art and science of routine can give us better lives, happier lives, more purposeful lives, but we also need instability and uncertainty to become greater than we ever imagined.

Acknowledgments

The book owes its existence to many people and particularly to my wife, Lisa, and my brother, Mario, who provide an honest assessment of the world we live in and our human nature. My journey in life has been touched by the mentorship and wisdom of not only the individuals in the world of philosophy, medicine, and corporate business, but also by charitable organizations, such as Direct Relief, that create a better world.

Index